Dad, for your love, your inspiration and your
continuing guidance

ST JUDE'S

GEMMA SISIA

MACMILLAN
Pan Macmillan Australia

First published 2007 in Macmillan by Pan Macmillan Australia Pty Limited
1 Market Street, Sydney

Reprinted 2007 (twice), 2008, 2009

National Library of Australia
Cataloguing-in-Publication data:

Sisia, Gemma.
St Jude's : a girl from Guyra, a school in Africa and the
patron saint of hopeless causes.

ISBN 9781405037952 (pbk).

1. School of St. Jude (Tanzania, Africa). 2. Schools –
Tanzania. 3. Education – Tanzania. I. Title. II. Title :
Saint Jude's : a girl from Guyra, a school in Africa and
the patron saint of hopeless causes

372.9678

Typeset in 12/16 pt Janson by Midland Typesetters, Australia
Printed by McPherson's Printing Group

Papers used by Pan Macmillan Australia Pty Ltd are natural, recyclable products made from
wood grown in sustainable forests. The manufacturing processes conform to the environmental
regulations of the country of origin.

ACKNOWLEDGEMENTS

As much as I would love to, it is impossible to name everyone who deserves to be thanked, because the acknowledgements would end up longer than the story. However, I have to say a special thank you to Sophie Lance, who took my stories, thoughts and ideas and translated them so brilliantly onto the page. Without her constant encouragement and support in so many ways, this book would never have been written. Thanks also to Tom Gilliatt at Pan Macmillan for his enthusiasm, commitment and passion for the book.

To Agnes Hanna, thanks for that first $10 you gave me to open the 'School Building Account'. Who would have ever thought it would come to fruition as it has?

Thanks so much to all the past and present Rotarians and District Governors of Rotary clubs and districts in so many parts of the world for helping my dream get off the ground. I have discovered what an extraordinary institution Rotary is – how many lives have been positively changed, children educated, families supported and diseases eradicated around the world. Keep going and never give up, for you are giving hope to people in almost every town in the world.

To all the individuals, families, service clubs, church groups, schools, institutions and businesses who help to sponsor our wonderful students, staff, buses and infrastructure, thank you.

To Gordon and Helen Smith, Mark and Amanda Cubit, Peter and Catherine Campbell, Tom and Judy Wagner, Rosemary and the late Laurie Breen, Paul and Margaret Weinland and all your families, thank you so much for your genuine love for and support of this project. Because of you, more children will be able to see the fulfilment of their dream – to one day proudly wear the St Jude's uniform.

To Richard Pagaliaro and all who help in maintaining the

website and the accounting systems, thank you. To think that only a year ago we didn't have a website – you have helped bring us into the 21st century.

Thank you to Kevin Pike and all at Roberts and Morrow in Armidale. I bet when you offered to audit our books for free, Kevin, you never thought you were going to take on such a big project!

To John Bailey and family. You have never stopped giving and you have never stopped looking out for the best interests of the school. You are true St Jude's family members.

Monica Hart, what can I say . . . you are the backbone of this school. Without your work in Australia, this school would never have got off the ground. We will be eternally indebted to you for your kindness to others.

To all the past and present staff and volunteers of the School of St Jude, thank you for putting up with the primitive conditions in the early days; thank you for your hard work and being flexible, tolerant, patient and prepared to try new ideas. You truly are the greatest team ever. I salute you for your work ethic and solid belief in the ethos of the school.

To my Kim, Charlotte, Karin, Mary, Maria, Nestory and Ben, it's only thanks to you that this school runs so beautifully. You are all full of character, heart, strength, commonsense and love for this project and I thank St Jude for bringing you here.

To my mum, Sue, brothers Tim, James, Nick, Benn, Matthew, Paddy and Danny, and all my wonderful sisters-in-law and family, thanks for making me who I am, because without you as my family I would not have had the guts to make this school a reality.

To my wonderful mother- and father-in-law and family. Thank you for being so accepting of my ideas and ways. You have helped me over so many obstacles and are always there for me.

Finally, to Richard, Nathaniel and Jackob. Words cannot explain how much I love you. You are always ready to make me laugh and to give me another push of encouragement or hug of support. Thank you for being mine.

INTRODUCTION

December 2005

It's early December at the School of St Jude and the school year is drawing to a close. It should be the start of the short wet season but the rains have been unreliable for the last few years and we're on the verge of drought. Each day, clouds gather overhead, bringing welcome relief from the heat; sometimes there's even a rumble of thunder, but mostly they just break up and drift off. Everything looks tired and parched. The grass beneath the pepper trees – a little reminder of home – has browned off and been ground into the soil by hundreds of hard-playing feet.

From my office, I can see the kids kicking a soccer ball around on the football fields beyond. As they scramble for the goal, they kick up swirls of chocolate-brown dust, dust which will turn instantly to thick claggy mud the moment we get a sniff of rain. If it comes.

The children are playing in front of the two big double-storey classroom blocks. Mount Meru floats behind them, its craggy volcanic cone disappearing into the high clouds as it mostly does

1

at this time of year. In front of them is the school hall, high-roofed and open-sided, centre for our assemblies, parent meetings, concerts, communal lunches, tests. Next year, it will house a proper kitchen, to feed the 700 children who will be coming to school (500 from this year plus another 200 new littlies). At the moment, it's filled with the scent of freshly sawn timber, as a handful of wood *fundi*s – carpenters – work to build hundreds of desks and chairs for the new pupils.

I spot Athumani among the soccer players and walk over to greet him, crunching over the driveway's volcanic gravel.

'Well, Athumani. How are you?'

'Good afternoon, Mrs Richard. I am very well, thank you.' His solemn, handsome face brightens. He is our head boy and takes his responsibilities very seriously.

'How do you think you went in your exams?'

'*Phenomenally*,' he says.

I laugh and tousle his curly black head. We've been teaching the kids that 'good' is not the only adjective in English. In their first language, Swahili, there is only one response to *Habari* (how's it going?) and that's *nzuri* (good). When they began to learn English, they used the same colourless adjective in every situation. So we taught them 'phenomenal', 'awesome', 'spectacular' and 'superb', and now everything – their health, their sporting prowess, their maths results – gets a range of ecstatic responses.

'So will you buy me a drink if you don't pass?'

'Certainly, Mrs Richard. But I know I have gone spectacularly well, probably 100 percent.'

Athumani is one of my Standard 4s, the ones who started the school with me and break new ground each year as they graduate from class to class. The year they've just completed is the one when most Tanzanians finish with school for good. Across the country, the children must sit for a series of demanding external nation-wide examinations. If they fail, as 80 to 90 percent of the children do, that is the end of their school career. Aged nine or ten, they become part of the same great Tanzanian workforce – or *lack* of workforce – as their parents, pushing a cart along the street for a few shillings, or selling vegetables or *ugali* – maize porridge – at the markets to other people who have just as little spare money as they.

This is the background of the children who go to the School of St Jude. They live either in extreme rural poverty or garbage-ridden urban slums, with no running water, no electricity, often inadequate food and, worst of all, no hope for change. The few children who might have made it through the Standard 4 exams if they'd been at a government school would – all but 15 percent – be knocked out at the next cull, the Standard 7 exams. Even those who passed would rarely be able to get a place in the few overcrowded government high schools. Without education, vocational training or money, the children would be condemned to the same precarious, drudge-filled existence as their parents or tempted into a barely more lucrative life of crime.

All the signs for our first-ever Standard 4 exams are good. We've had the results from the trial exams and I suspect that all our children are not just going to pass but do really, really well.

As I look across at them playing, my heart fills with pride. I am, of course, biased, but they are an exceptional bunch of children and have come so far already. I can't wait to see what they make of their lives. Their ambitions are so lofty and I'll do everything in my power to help them achieve them.

There's skinny little Alex Elifas, playing with his friend Kevin. Alex is a gorgeous, hard-working boy, the youngest of many children. I know that things are often tight for him at home but his ambition when he grows up isn't to try to make his own life more comfortable, but to work with orphans whom he sees as having an even harder life than his own.

And Cecilia Benedict. She's a big, solid, smiley thing, able to look an adult in the eye and speak with confidence on any subject. I can see in her the dependable, caring minister she would one day like to be. When I look back to when these children started a few years ago, none of them could do more than mutter 'Good morning' at their shoes and now they speak English with amazing fluency.

Cecilia's friend, Esuvat Ojungo, is still a little shy around adults, but since she's been taking extracurricular drama, she's been growing in confidence every week. Esuvat is extremely self-motivated. In the new house her father has been building – no water or power but a big step up from a mud hut – she stays up late, long after her household chores are finished, studying by the light of a little kerosene lamp. She'd like to be a pilot – as would Athumani – or perhaps a news reporter. I reckon she could be anything she wanted.

And there's little Eliudi William, another one to watch, playing, as usual, with his big friend Pius, the tallest and – by far – oldest boy in the class. Eliudi is shy, a little unsure of himself and seems surprised by his own achievements at school. But he's got a real strength in science and I wouldn't be surprised if he does eventually become the meteorologist he says he would like to be. That is, if he doesn't hit the professional disco circuit – all the kids love it when Eliudi takes to the dance floor and shakes his groovy little tail.

These children and all the others in their year are so dear to me; we've been through so much together. In four years, we've grown from a school of three children to one of nearly 700. We've built classroom blocks, a library, an assembly hall, playing fields and we're still growing bigger and stronger. Every year at least 150 new children are able to come to St Jude's to receive the sort of education that would have been out of the reach of anyone in their family. And almost all the children attend the school totally free of charge, thanks to the hundreds of individuals, families, clubs, schools, classes and companies who sponsor the children here. What they receive is not just tuition but a good, hot, nutritious lunch, a uniform, stationery, textbooks, safe transport to and from home and, perhaps as important as anything else, the opportunity to be kids.

Here, they have a break from chores and the grim world of taking on adult responsibilities while they are still children. They are encouraged to swing on swings, kick a football, try their hand at drama, drumming, Scouts or Girl Guides, netball or table tennis. They have a chance to explore and develop, which should be every child's birthright.

If ever I wonder just why a country girl from Guyra, New South Wales, is living here in Africa, I have nearly 700 good reasons and counting.

CHAPTER ONE

I was going to be a boy. Everyone who knew the Rice family expected it. Mum and Dad had already had four in short succession – Tim, James, Nick and Benn – and Mum had resigned herself to a lifetime of big voices, big appetites and big laundry loads. Then, four years after Benn, I arrived.

My father, Basil, rang Mum's father, Stanley Moran, with the news. 'It's a girl!'

'You're kidding me, Basil, aren't you? I thought you were on your way to your own football team.'

'I promise you, it's a girl this time. We're calling her Gemma, after Saint Gemma Galgani, from Lucca in Italy.'

Unconvinced, my grandfather rang Armidale Hospital and only after receiving confirmation that, yes, a girl had been born to the Rices, she was a whopper and everything was fine, did he give a whoop and order an enormous bouquet of the finest pale pink roses for *his* little girl, who at last had a daughter of her own.

Poor Mum probably needed some female companionship in

her life. She did it tough out at our home in country New South Wales, though no one ever heard her complain. She was a city girl, from Brighton in Melbourne and, as she says, 'If your father had told me when he proposed that we would end up having eight children and living on a property, well, he would have had a lot more convincing to do before I said yes.' This was years later, when she also used to say: 'Embarrassment? I'm beyond embarrassment – I have eight children.' In the intervening years had come another boy, Matthew, two and a half years younger than me. Then, as if to underline the joke, at 44 Mum had identical twin boys, Paddy and Danny, nearly 20 years after her first child. She still says, apart from anything else, she could write a whole book on the twins alone.

It wasn't the future that either of them would have had in mind when they met at Melbourne University, Dad studying law and Mum physiotherapy. But then again they probably weren't typical city students. They were both devout Catholics with a sense of purpose and commitment beyond their immediate circumstances. They also set the benchmark for a family full of extreme sports nuts by spending their spare time at uni rally-driving, with Dad at the wheel and Mum navigating.

By the time I arrived, Dad had put aside his early career as a barrister and followed his dream to raise superfine wool merinos. After marrying in the chapel of Melbourne Uni's beautiful Newman College, where Dad had lived in 1959, Dad practised law till the mid-60s when he bought a large grazing property, Springmount, 10 kilometres east of a small town called Guyra on the top of the Great Dividing Range near Armidale, close to the New England Highway, in northern New South Wales. There he brought my mother and three older brothers to live, soon joined by Benn, then me, then Matthew. When I was about four, we settled at a property called Wyoming – a name which still sounds like home to me – 40 kilometres west of Guyra, about halfway between Inverell and Armidale.

It was a beautiful property, tucked at the end of a pine-lined road, with a rainbow trout-filled river that eventually flows into the Macintyre. We had 100,000 acres (here and elsewhere) supporting around 80,000 sheep at the height of wool production, not to mention cattle, chickens and a fluctuating population of horses to serve the purposes of eight horse-mad children.

Mum's and Dad's domains were very separate: Mum had the homestead and the garden, Dad the property beyond. Mum was a perfectionist, a difficult thing when you're living in the bush with eight fairly wild children, seven of them boys. She set a standard for civilised, ethical living and made sure we always lived up to that standard.

My mother ran the house beautifully, created a magical garden and pushed us to be much more than your typical family of country yokels. She was an incredible gardener with a big vision and she did everything herself. She'd build rockeries and grottos, rose gardens and arches. One year she made Dad a big rain gauge with a two-foot square rock base, where most people would stick a plastic tube against a wall and call it quits. Her floral arrangements have always been in great demand as well, for weddings, balls and funerals. That's what Mum was like with everything: she gave it all 110 percent and her resulting garden became a local attraction.

Nowadays, if you had that many children, everyone would be amazed if they were even fed and dressed. But when we were growing up, we had eggs for breakfast, cooked lunches, clothes run up on the sewing machine. When we were sick, we'd be propped up in bed with jelly, mashed banana, ice cream and lemonade. There'd always be a soup or a stew simmering on the stove. The boys would kill two or three sheep a week and when they were learning to butcher their own meat there would always be wonky cuts for the pot. My mother was such a 'mum'.

When you're dealing with numbers like ours, everything has to be run with military precision. For breakfast, we'd line up for our cereal and egg (both compulsory), then move round to the sink where we had our milk – chocolate for the boys and for me strawberry, one of my few nods to girliness. Breakfast was the one meal I didn't have to set the table for – Mum would have already set it with ten different cereals. By the time we came in for breakfast, Mum would be standing by the stoves (we had two to cater for the family), dishing out eggs.

'How many for you, Gem?'

'Two please, Mum.'

'Benn?'

'Four please, Mum.'

Dinners were run on the same lines. Mum dished out a scoop of mashed potatoes, a couple of spoonfuls of peas and a number of lamb chops to each child, dependent on their age and sex. The bigger the boy, the more chops he received – Benn regularly put away seven! The older boys' plates were arrayed near the plate warmer, then, winding around the kitchen bench, came the younger children's plates in order, till the room was circled by plates filled with decreasing numbers of chops.

No one could leave the table until everyone's plate was clean. The older boys would be waiting as we younger children dawdled over our vegies, and more than once James would threaten Matt and me: 'You've got till the big hand gets to the ten to finish. Otherwise, I'm going to hit ya.' We'd gulp it down pretty quick. Anything we couldn't stomach was tucked under the table on a ledge that is probably still decorated with dried lumps of old vegies.

We wanted to be outside, you see. Our world was the property and all the things it offers a child: riding horses and motorbikes, trout fishing, swimming in waterfalls. And hard work, of course. We all had chores, practically from the moment we could toddle outside with a load of scraps for the chooks. By the time I went to school in Inverell, I would have been putting in a couple of hours before the school bus came at 7.30, feeding the horses, letting them out and exercising them. Like most children if they're given the chance, I preferred animals to toys. My mother and grandmother Nan Moran lovingly sewed countless little dolls' outfits for me, but they might as well have saved their efforts – I had no interest in dolls.

My first pet was a little wild mouse. I carried it everywhere with me and one day, when I was in the wheat silo, I lost it. A mouse in a wheat silo is probably a very happy mouse but it was a very lost mouse and I wept tragically. Mrs Ray, who sometimes looked after us and was sort of a surrogate grandmother, found me.

'Whatever's the matter, child?'

'I've lost my mouse, I've lost my mouse,' I sobbed.

She smiled and reached to pat my hair . . . and plucked out the mouse which was resting comfortably in my wild curls.

After the mouse, the first real animal of my own was a horse, when I was about four. I'd been riding since I was a baby in nappies, being helped by Dad onto Dutchess's back for a photo. She was a wonderful horse, white, with shining black hooves and a dark grey mane, and she'd follow me round wherever I went. She wasn't like that for everyone. In fact, if anyone else tried to sit on her, she'd try to jam their leg against the closest tree, so Dad could only show her in the 'led' categories at the shows. But for me, Dutchess was as dependable as an old dog.

By the time I was three or four, I was learning to jump. One of my very first strong memories is from around that time. Dad, who was well known for his showjumping coaching, used to go to the Guyra pony camp each year to teach the local boys and girls how to jump. At the time we had a horse who'd been named Magician because he had once jumped through a barn window and had miraculously survived. Magician was a real character – you could never catch him, he'd just jump away. You'd put him in a yard, he'd jump the fence, you'd put him in a stable, he'd jump the door. You'd put him in one paddock and he'd jump to another where the grass was better.

Of course, he was completely unsuitable for a four-year-old, strong in the mouth and headstrong with it. My older brothers could ride him but not me. But this one time, Dad sat me on Magician and fixed a lunge on to him so that he could stand in the middle and lead me on Magician around him in a circle. First we did a little circuit. Then he put out a couple of drums so that Magician could do a little jump, then another couple and another. Eventually the jumps were at about five or six foot, Magician soaring over them like a bird, and me holding on and laughing with excitement and the total pleasure of the sensation.

From then on, nothing could hold me back. We had a little showground on the farm and every day Dad would give me a lesson. Benn and Matthew exercised their horses while I had my lesson, then we'd swap over, so we all had some time alone with Dad, which was very precious. All of us loved to ride. Between us, we've covered some pretty extreme sports: rodeos, bull-riding, hang-gliding, light planes, pyrogliding, ship-diving. We're all challenge junkies to an extent. I can see that it's still a big part of what drives me. At home, we had a trophy wall covered with our various ribbons and awards, everything from certificates from local elocution competitions to trophies won while representing the state.

In our family, every little thing would be turned into a competition. Like when we'd catch the bus in the morning for school.

The bus would come all the way out to our farm to take us to Holy Trinity, the little Catholic school in Inverell, and stop for us on the other side of the cattle grid. We were allowed to ride our bikes down the hill and hide them behind the big pine tree. I had my green pushbike but Benn – oh, the unfairness of it – had a homemade minibike, put together by Dad with a little ingenuity and a couple of lawn mower wheels.

On the downhill run, I had the advantage – pedals and suspension – but Benn would always overtake me on the way back up. As time went on, the course became more elaborate and competitive. You had to park your bike, jump the cattle grid, jump over the log, touch the big rock and whoever made it first to the tree was the winner. Benn would always beat me during the last leg. On the few occasions I made it first to the tree, Benn would suddenly announce a change in the course – another log that had to be climbed over, or a reversal of the order of rock and tree. Very annoying.

Did the young me think, *Oh well, he's a boy, he's almost five years older than me, let's forget about it*? I *don't* think so! I decided that the way for me to win was to beat him not to the finish line but the starting line. I snuck off at 5.30 in the morning and did the whole obstacle race, down the hill, across the cattle grid, over the log, round the rock and touch the tree. When I didn't show up at six o'clock for breakfast, Mum and Dad and the boys set off to look for me. They found me, panting but triumphant, by the pine tree: 'Beat ya, Benn!'

The look in his eyes was pitying. 'No, Gemma, I think you'll find you haven't won because you went *over* the log, not *under* it. I'm afraid you're disqualified.'

But going to the agricultural shows, we were all in it together. It was a real family activity that united us, whatever our age or sex. On Fridays, I'd usually be given the day off school. Being a country school, it wasn't really out of the ordinary. We'd wash and groom the horses and put them in the big truck and hitch up our super-sized caravan and off we'd go. If it was March, we'd head across to Bingara Show, Warialda Show and onto Moree Show. Then Easter was taken up by the big Sydney show, and so on. You were with your family the whole time and that's what made it so great. Wonderful Dad was also the president of the Showman's Guild and so we would have a handful of free tickets for various sideshows, which added to our fun.

Around where we lived, there were lots of big families like ours who were into horses and we'd all meet up at the same shows – the Chaffeys, Harveys, Johnsons, Ferrys, Straleys, Botfields and Hoffmans. It was sort of a club. The kids would sleep in the caravans or trucks or, when they were old enough, they'd bed down with the horses. We'd all compete in the events and go round the sideshows. I did a bit of hacking but my main event was showjumping and I actually competed in the annual NSW State Championships from when I was nine until I went to boarding school at 16.

It was a fantastic experience. I think one of the reasons Mum and Dad encouraged us to compete was that it taught us independence and responsibility for our own actions. We had to feed our horses, wash them, look after our saddle gear. When you were out competing, you had to learn to make decisions quickly and then live with those decisions.

One of those other big country families at the shows was the Hiscox family, who had a son a couple of years older than me who – naturally – became my first boyfriend. Russell and I had a very cute relationship, all very innocent. We were always chasing each other round the showground and were ever on the lookout for ways to make money to spend on rides and sideshows.

We were at the local Guyra Show when Russ said to me:

'Hey, Gem, you want to go on the Wizard?' (This was our sideshow ride of choice at the time.)

'Sure, Russ, but I'm out of money.'

'No worries,' he said. 'Let's go in the rescue relay and win some.'

The rescue relay was a riding event you entered in pairs. The first person had to jump every fence as fast as they could and, if they made a mistake, the second person would come in and continue the race. The team that successfully cleared the most jumps in the given time won. We'd usually make enough money from events like this to go on a few rides and buy some rubbish.

On this particular occasion, in the wild action of the relay, I had a really bad fall. I headed towards a jump and my horse didn't even attempt to lift his legs. He just went straight through it and fell, with me underneath him. I used to fall off my horse about two or three times a week and it never worried me, but this was one of the two times when I had to be hospitalised.

The first bad accident had been on our farm a few years before. We were coming back from our next door neighbours', the Jacksons, where we'd had a swim in their pool – it was so great that they had a pool, much better than our waterfalls, we thought – and the horse I was riding, Dad's horse Dion, took off. My father always said, if a horse bolts, just pull on one rein. They'll have to go in smaller and smaller circles and eventually stop. He also said that Dion liked to test his riders – well, this was a test and a half!

I pulled and pulled on one rein and the horse veered to the left, but instead of stopping we just came closer and closer to the barbed wire fence that separated the sheep paddocks. Dion, being a great jumper, decided that, rather than letting the fence get in his way, he'd jump it instead. Somehow his feet got caught on the top wire, he somersaulted the fence and took me with him. I did a somersault over Dion's head as well and that's all I can remember until I woke up in hospital. In years to come, Dion was the only horse Dad would ride around the stock. He lasted well into his thirties – a very great age for a horse – until he fell into the sheep dip and had to be put down. Dad never rode a horse again.

The fall at the Guyra Show while I was competing with Russell was probably more serious. Thankfully I was wearing a helmet, but the helmet was cracked like an egg, which gave me a nasty idea of what might have happened to my skull if it hadn't been protected. Mum, who'd been watching from the sidelines, jumped the fence and raced over to where I was lying, motionless and unbreathing. She tried to resuscitate me and I was taken to hospital unconscious but breathing. The other horsey show families were so good to us, making sure that all our horses were looked after – fed, watered and rugged – while my family stayed by my side in hospital.

After that, I was supposed to have a rest from riding for a few months. By this stage I was a very committed rider and it was the Queensland Showjumping Championships three months later. I really, *really* wanted to go. The doctors didn't want me to, Mum didn't want me to, but Dad, bless him, said, 'Let her go, she is really ready for this.' Little did I know, but when we went up to the competition, Mum went straight to the hospital and then worked out the quickest route between there and the show-ground, just in case.

Although I was only fourteen, I had to compete in the A-grade category. Usually, I would be in the C-grade: B-grade was for 15–17-year-olds and A was for 17–21-year-olds. But in Queens-land they graded the horse, not the rider, and my horse, Moonman (named for his sky-high jumps), had been given an

A-grade ranking based on his past performance. This was great ammunition for Mum to stop me from entering, but Dad stood firm and said that we hadn't driven all the way to Queensland for nothing and, at the very least, I would compete in the Grand Prix showjumping event (in which there weren't many jumps, but the height of each was raised round after round until all but one competitor were knocked out).

I was fine. Better than fine. Moonman and I just clicked and I won. I'll never forget Mum's tears and Dad's joy: first place at the Queensland State Championships. The ribbon is still on the wall in the family room at Wyoming, along with the family's other special ribbons and trophies. I think a library of books could be written just about the stories behind the mementos and trophies in our family room.

Not long after this, I was in the supermarket with Mum when a middle-aged man approached us.

'Hello, Mrs Rice, Gemma. Good to you see you on your feet.'

I looked enquiringly at Mum, having never seen this man before in my life.

'This is Mr Kelly, the ambulance driver, Gemma. The reason you don't recognise him is that every time you meet, you're actually unconscious, but he knows you a bit too well. Say "thank you" to Mr Kelly.'

'Thank you, Mr Kelly', I said politely.

The Sydney show – the Royal Easter Show – was a highlight and it showed Dad at his inventive best. Dad was a bit like Mum in that everything he did received his full attention and effort, but he was impatient as well, like me. Things had to have been done yesterday, but with him they also had to be done right. Dad started out as president of our little Guyra Show. Under his ten-year leadership, he brought the Zonal Show Girls competition to the town, then the New South Wales and even the National Rodeo Championships. Dad became zone president, then ended up President of the NSW Agricultural Societies Committee Showman's Guild and also Vice President of the Royal Agricultural Society, which runs the Sydney Royal Easter Show.

He was also very creative. Sydney was such a big show that you weren't allowed to take your trucks and caravans into the showground – in those days at Moore Park – but you had to park around neighbouring Centennial Park and walk your horses in. However, before Dad became well known we'd always come to the front gate of the showground, in our extra-large horse truck, towing the extended two-door caravan. It was at a T-junction on a busy city road so our little convoy had the potential to create quite a traffic jam.

Dad had this old straw hat under the seat and he'd jam it down low on his head. 'Okay, kids, let's see if we can get into the showground with this truck and horses.'

With our mouths hanging open and eyeballs rolling, we'd watch Dad cut across the intersection into one of the gates, blocking off a good three lanes of traffic. All the cars would be hooting and the gatesman would come out shouting and waving his arms.

'Hey, mister, you're not allowed to take your truck in here. You should know that.'

Dad would look like he was chewing the cud. 'Oim from up Goira way. Gee I dunno how oim gunna back out of this one.' Meanwhile horns were blaring and people were yelling from their cars and trucks in the three lanes of traffic that Dad had successfully blocked.

'Oh, gee, oh, oh, all right, come in quick before the police come over and shut us down,' the gatesman would say in exasperation. And every year that's how we got the truck into the Sydney Showground.

Dad's creative genius came to the fore at another show – this time, the Brisbane Show, where I was supposed to be competing in the Under-15 Pairs event with a boy from Glen Innes called Brent McLeod. In the Pairs, working as a team is everything: not only are you supposed to ride in tandem, in as similar a manner as possible, but your horses should even look alike. Brent and I really wanted to win but we weren't hopeful, as we knew we would be competing against the best from all over Queensland and our horses were disadvantaged from the start by being slightly different colours: mine light brown, Brent's dark.

Brent's father, Max, and Dad put their heads together – they were great friends – and came up with the ingenious solution of dyeing my horse to match Brent's. One day we had a mismatch and the next, a perfectly matched pair, which we rode to victory.

It must have been hard for Mum. I'm sure she would have liked me to be a bit more physically cautious and also to help out more in the house but, with seven brothers, not only did *they* forget I was a girl, *I* forgot I was a girl. I was expected to muster cattle, mark lambs, put rings around their balls and tails, pull them out of their labouring mothers and pick up dead sheep for the dump. The only job I was not encouraged to do was help dip the sheep, because Dad said the toxic chemicals could possibly affect any future children I might have.

Everyone works hard on the land. It's the same all over the world and it never occurs to you that anyone's life is any different. Most of my friends at primary school were from similar backgrounds, like Kylee Ticehurst, one of my two best friends when I was young. Kylee's family were wheat farmers out near

Inverell, another big Catholic family. Her big brother Paul was great mates with my big brother Benn, her little brother Michael was great mates with my little brother Matthew, and so on. My other close friend was Anthea Boulus, who was a town girl. We'd always stay at her place if there was something on at school at night or a social, because we lived an hour out of town. She must have been a bit tougher than most of the town girls because we didn't really have much in common with most of them. If one of them fell off a motorbike or something, they were likely to start crying. We'd just dust ourselves off and jump back on and Anthea was always ready to have a go. Also, town girls got their kicks from activities like walking around town looking at shops, which left me underwhelmed. Hadn't I discovered at home how very wonderful it was to bring up my own baby animals?

The first baby animal I reared on my own was when I was about eight or nine. It was lambing season, during spring, and I was out with Dad in the old Nissan four-wheel drive doing our usual check of the ewes that were lambing. Every now and then we'd find one having difficulties and have to help deliver the lamb. On the side of the hill in Reedy Creek paddock, there was one ewe whose lamb was clearly stuck.

'Go on, Gem, go and pull the lamb,' said Dad.

I pulled and out flopped a small, lifeless bundle. Disappointing, but a fact of life. I was getting ready to roll the ewe down the hill, which helped loosen them up after they'd been lying down so long struggling with childbirth, when another head popped out.

'Dad! She's having twins! Maybe this one will be alive.' But it was as blue and still as its brother. Again, I prepared to roll the ewe. But she wasn't finished – a third head popped out. This time I pulled out a perfect, though small, lamb, alive. The poor ewe at this stage had lost whatever interest she might have had in the proceedings and wandered off, so Dad said I could have the lamb.

I called him Reedy and he was gorgeous. I used to feed him so much milk that his stomach would bloat. Due to absolute over-indulgence he ended up really short and stunted, but he was the animal that got me on the track to running a nursery.

Once I realised how great it was to hand-rear baby animals, I was always on the lookout for orphaned lambs. Sometimes, not quite orphaned. I'd spot one that looked cute and if it wasn't actually attached to a mother I'd bring it back to Dad. 'Dad, I've found another orphan.' By the time I'd collected about 30 lambs, Dad twigged to what I was doing. He told me that I wasn't to take any more lambs and I had to give at least half of the ones I already had to Stumpy, an old man from Ben Lomond who lived about 30 minutes up the road. For months afterwards when we took the shortcut through Ben Lomond, I'd look out for my lambs at the back of Stumpy's house.

Another time, it was lambing season and the lambs were all new when there was a snap freeze over one weekend. All over the property there were lambs either dead or frozen half to death. I went around on one of my brothers' motorbikes – even though I was expected to do all the stockwork like the boys, I was never given a gun or a motorbike like them, grrrrrr – and collected as many as I could that still had a breath of life in them.

I thought, *Where would be the best place to warm them up?* It seemed to me that Mum's formal sitting room, with its nice open fire and velvet seats and marble tables, was an excellent choice. What could be a better sight than 40 baby lambs sitting around the fireplace, warming their little woolly heads? Well, most things, actually, according to my mother.

'This is not a barnyard, Gemma!' she said, and she was pretty angry. 'This is my one good room in the whole house!' Still, Mum gave in to the big heart she has for sick animals and people, and relented. She even helped me get some milk into them to give some a chance of survival. Even with warmth and milk, some were doomed. I don't know why, but once a lamb starts to stretch its head all the way to the back, you just know it's going to die, no matter what treatment it receives.

Then one day, the boys had all the cattle in the yard and one of the cows had a calf while they were in there. This isn't ideal and often the mother will reject the calf in these circumstances. Dad came up to the house and said: 'I've got a calf down in the yard, Gemma. The mother's gone a bit mad. Would you be interested in raising it?'

Would I? I was down there like a shot to pick up my beautiful little jet-black calf whose name, I decided, would be Gus.

Being a newborn, Gus was bottle-fed at first but soon he moved on to lapping his milk from an old drench container that I had cut in half and cleaned. Dad told me that calves still needed to have a sucking action or else they wouldn't develop an important enzyme: it's not like a dog or a cat who can drink from a bowl without a problem as soon as they can physically manage it. So after Gus had drunk his milk, I'd sit there for about five minutes with him sucking on my thumb. As he got bigger and bigger, I'd put a few fingers in, then my whole hand, all to get his enzymes going. By this stage, I'd be sitting on his back while he sucked, my feet just touching the ground. Gradually, my feet began to lift off the ground, but still Gus, who was now a bull, liked to suckle on my whole hand. As he got older, his tongue rasped like sandpaper.

This was all very cute but it occurred to me that I could put his tameness to good use. I'd seen a television program about a girl who taught a steer to jump because her parents wouldn't buy her a horse. *Cool*, I thought. *I'll give it a go with Gus, even though he's a bull, not a steer.*

The next day I led an uncomplaining Gus over to the stables.

I tried to put a bridle on him but his big head was too fat for the headband so I had to readjust the whole thing before I put the saddle on him. I jumped on, stuck my hand in his mouth as a lure and gave him a kick. He didn't move. Poor Gus stood there like a big, overgrown baby as I rummaged in my brother Nick's rodeo bag for a tool. He had a nasty pair of spurs. *Yep, these will make him move*, I thought. So I strapped them on, leaped on his back and let him have it.

Yeehah! He moved all right. By the time he'd stopped bucking, I was sprawling in the dirt, dishevelled and not knowing exactly where I was. I figured that teaching a bull to showjump perhaps wasn't a realistic ambition and that Gus was better off just being a bull. Actually, he never fathered a calf so he wasn't much good at that either, so he ended up at the abattoir (I was away at school at the time). He was cute, though, and taught me a lot about duty and responsibility.

A world away from showjumping and the farm, I had another, very different, life, entirely instigated by my mother. Oddly enough, it couldn't have been better preparation for what I do now. From the age of four, I used to go 80 kilometres into Armidale once a week for elocution lessons with a gorgeous old nun called Mother Xavier. For Mum, it wasn't enough that we were fed and healthy and (more or less) schooled. We had to be culturally well-rounded as well. So off we trotted for elocution and drama, guitar and piano. I even did ballet for a brief, misguided time. But elocution – learning to speak confidently in front of any audience – I loved.

Old Mother Xavier would sit behind her big old wooden convent desk and make us recite poems. She made up special little poems for me and Matthew, like 'I hate porridge, it makes me sick' and one about 'a drip called James and a drop called Nick'. Once I started going to school, Mum would take us to every eisteddfod in the district, competing in poetry and drama and sight-reading. Being the competitive animal that I am, I thrived on it and did very well.

As I got older, I moved from Mother Xavier to Mrs Fraser, who was the most exacting teacher imaginable. For $1.60 an hour she would pull our poetry or prose recital to shreds. I never had a lesson without criticism. Later on, when I was at boarding school in Sydney I had a $50-an-hour elocution teacher who listened to whatever I recited and said, 'That's lovely, Gemma, thank you.' Then I'd go home on the holidays to Mrs Fraser so she could rip me apart again to help me improve my work. She was wonderful. Considering I now have to raise almost all the money for St Jude's through public speaking, I couldn't have had a better foundation.

Mum also told us that we had each to learn a musical instrument. Mine – and I hated it – was the piano. When I was in First Grade, Mum used to pick me up from school and drop me off to my teacher, a very strict nun at the Sisters of Mercy in Inverell. I was terrified of her and far too frightened to ask where the toilet was when, one lesson, I needed to use it. Instead, I just wet my pants, which the Sister didn't notice until a puddle had spread on the wooden boards beneath the piano. Mum then moved me to the wonderfully kind, patient Mrs Hamilton, who was so nice that I got away with doing little practice or playing all year. In the weeks before my annual exams, I would madly learn every piece by heart and cram all the theory and end up passing well – though the pressure made poor Mrs Hamilton older and greyer.

We were always encouraged to perform publicly. One time, Matthew and I were dragged by Mum to the local eisteddfod in Inverell to compete in the junior piano duet. We sat low in our seats ready for the competition and would have given anything not to have been there. Then we were saved – maybe someone upstairs thought we'd been through purgatory enough. A woman came up to Mum and told her that our father had just rung to say that he hadn't seen the twins in the five hours since we'd left home.

Mum grabbed Matthew and me and threw us into the car. Even though we were an hour from home, Mum set a record that day which has yet to be broken, making the trip in 20 minutes flat. The twins were so independent because they had each other that they were always going missing and we often had to raise official search parties to find them. I think that's one of the reasons my mum went prematurely grey. Eventually my elder brother James found the twins in their nappies more than a kilometre from the house, 'going to catch yabbies' in the biggest dam on the property! I was just pleased to get out of the piano competition. It was a happy day for me when Mum and Dad said I could give up the piano when I left for boarding school.

Thursday was our day for extracurricular activities and it was also Mum's shopping and errand day in town. Mum would pick us all up from school in the station wagon then whip around, dropping and picking us up at ballet, football, netball, drama, piano, the doctor, the dentist. We'd always finish up at Coles, where we each were given a trolley to look after. Mum would regularly fill five trolleys and leave them at the end of the rows, ready for us to race them to the checkout. Eventually, we would get back to the farm with melted ice cream and half-eaten bread loaves at about 9 pm to be welcomed by Dad's weekly Thursday-night dish of spaghetti and meat sauce. It would take Mum another clear hour to unload all the groceries into the cupboards. I don't think I'll ever be able to be the supermum that she was every minute of her life while we were growing up. She really was amazing.

Because of my involvement in showjumping and public speaking, I was able to delay going off to boarding school until my final two years of high school. Most of the boys went in Year 9. Holy Trinity school in Inverell finished at Year 10, so for years 11 and 12 I had to move to Sydney to St Vincent's College in Potts Point. Mum and Dad sacrificed so much to give all of us a private education and St Vincent's was at that time the sister school of St Joseph's College in Hunter's Hill where all the boys went.

The older boys had grown up by the time I went to Sydney. Tim had studied law, like Dad, but he'd always had a strong religious side and had considered the priesthood. Even when Tim was little, he'd do James and Nick's chores for them rather than see them in trouble. He's always been a sweetheart like that, almost too thoughtful for his own good. James, who's a wild boy, had been a reluctant student but Dad insisted that all of us have some qualification, saying that farming was too difficult to rely on. So James went to Longreach Agricultural College in Queensland, and got a pilot's licence as well. He's a very successful banker now. Nick – another reluctant student – had gone into a very tough building industry apprenticeship and was on his way to being a Clerk of Works. Today he's a big developer around our home towns of Armidale and Inverell and is set for an early retirement, with his fine wife, Yvonne, and two sons. Both James and Nick were still heavily into rodeo-riding – Nick was placed third in the world in bull-riding in his prime. His mementos join my ribbons on the wall in our family room at the farm.

My dear brother Benn, whom I was probably closest to all the time we were growing up, was never very academic. But he's always been the human relations king – you could drop him into any situation and he'd instantly make friends. Everyone loved him and he was everyone's mate. We did everything together. After Year 12, he went up to Alice Springs and studied hotel management. He lives in Armidale now with his wife, Bianca, and three children, and helps Mum manage Wyoming, as well as lecturing at the local TAFE.

So now it was my turn to leave home. I'd already had some thoughts about what I wanted to do later, when I would leave school. For the last couple of years, the famine in Ethiopia had been big news, with Bob Geldof and Live Aid bringing the world's attention to one of its often forgotten corners. We were saturated with images of starving children, their little bellies distended and tragic eyes big in their oversized heads.

I'm not an overtly emotional person and I still can't see much use in sitting around crying about something but I decided, really as soon as I started seeing those pictures, that I would one day go to work in Africa, to help people in need, in whatever capacity I could.

It seemed a natural progression for me. At home, Mum and Dad had an open-door policy and were always helping someone out. As soon as they moved to Springmount, my parents immediately involved themselves in the local community, hosting clubs in their shearers' quarters and helping to run everything from the local soccer club to Scouts to the debutante balls. Community is at the heart of country life and, as a young couple, Mum and Dad's activities meant they were intimately involved with their fellow country folk at every level, from families doing it tough right up to Australia's Governor-General, Lord Casey, whom they entertained at home in March 1966.

Mum became a member of the Armidale View Club and charter president of the Quota women's service club, and went on to establish a local senior citizens' club. Even when he was no longer practising as a lawyer, Dad often gave free legal advice to any workers who were down on their luck. We always kept spare mattresses on the verandah for anyone who needed a bed for the night and Dad gave jobs to people – usually local Aboriginal fellas – even if they'd had trouble with the law or with grog. There would sometimes be an alcoholic staying at the shearers' quarters while they tried to clean themselves up, and we often had a few extras at dinner.

It never occurred to me that there was anything unusual about this but certainly my parents were a big influence on me, especially as we were living in the country so far out of town. At the time, I thought everyone's life was exactly the same – I'd certainly never met anyone who just tried to amass money and possessions without returning anything to the community. It wasn't the way people did things.

At the back of my parents' behaviour, I suppose, was a Christian concept of serving your fellow man. My parents brought us all up as strict Catholics, something that still lies at the heart of everything I do. When I was growing up, there was no question of missing a Sunday mass, no matter what rodeo or show we were at. We'd always find a church for Sunday or, if we were close enough, we'd try to make it back home. Mum and Dad had lots of really close friends who were priests or worked in other religious capacities and we'd often have them for the weekend. There was one gorgeous retired bishop, Bishop Kennedy, who'd been the Bishop of Armidale for many years. He'd come to us for a weekend every month, just to have a break from his retirement home. Another, Father Pat, was a vivacious old Irish priest who'd gone into retirement in Brisbane. Then there was Father Ferdie, a Franciscan priest, who'd worked building schools in Papua New Guinea for 25 years and then for St Vincent de Paul in Brisbane, looking after the down and out who used to seek him out as he sat for hours on a seat at a bus stop.

All of these men had a great influence on me, but ours wasn't the stilted, formal relationship you might imagine between children and a priest. They were just great people to have around and formed the backbone of our 'Wyoming Family', which developed from a casual network into an official organisation so that other people like these great men could come together to pray, relax and support each other in a loving environment. My grandfathers had died when I was really little, so Bishop Kennedy was like a grandfather to me, always a great listener and full of good ideas. Father Pat was more like another big brother – you could chuck a tea towel at him and say, 'Go on, Father Pat, get cracking on the dishes.' And Father Ferdie helped transform my vague dreams of going to Africa into concrete plans and was full of experience and wisdom from his time in New Guinea.

As these visits became more and more regular, Dad actually fixed up an altar in the dining room so that the priests could say mass. We began a tradition of hosting a 'First Friday' – a Catholic devotion – every month. The Wyoming Family attracted new members all the time, and it was great to have so many people genuinely caring about you. By this stage, the older boys were grown up and great travellers, as are we all. Wherever they went, they'd send back a religious souvenir or two for Mum and Dad which would go into the dining room. So the dining room gradually became a chapel, full of religious ornaments and mementos from Lourdes and Fatima, Mount Sinai and Bethlehem. Actually, I can't remember it ever having been used as a dining room.

So that's the background from which I went down to boarding school, to St Vincent's in Potts Point, in the heart of Sydney's infamous Kings Cross area. I was conservative, religious, *very* serious about studying – I'd decided the best way to help in Africa was by being a doctor – but, funnily enough, not all that insular or particularly shockable. My parents had made sure we all spent enough time in the city before moving there for school – they didn't want us gawking around, tripping over our own feet, looking at skyscrapers. Travelling wasn't a problem for me because I'd been doing it for so many years with the horses and shows and we'd all been brought up to be outgoing and embrace new adventures.

I was ready for this one.

CHAPTER TWO

I dived straight into boarding school and thrived. Possibly too well – without the horses to exercise and with all that good stodgy boarding school food, not to mention sitting around on my bum studying, I piled on a huge amount of weight in my first term. It was a great time for me: debating, going out, enjoying my first time of living in the city and being able to pop out to the movies or the occasional pub on the weekend.

I made a couple of very close friends – Leasa Mays in particular with whom I still keep in touch – and we had a lot of fun. But at the back of my mind, I always knew I was there to study and I worked as hard as possible. Getting into medicine meant everything to me. Also I was very aware that it was a struggle to send eight children to private boarding schools on a farmer's income and I wanted to be worthy of my parents' sacrifice.

My parents were great believers in the importance of education. They would say: 'You could have a brand new car and crash it tomorrow. You could lose your farm. You could buy a new house and have it burn to the ground overnight. But nothing –

not disaster, not drought, not a bad government – can take your education away from you.' It was firmly instilled in me then, and I believe it more than ever now.

Living in Potts Point was an education in itself. To get to sport or debating, we'd always catch the train and our way to the station was through the heart of the red light district. There were pimps and touts hustling outside every doorway.

'Say a prayer for the evil ones, girls,' they'd yell as we trotted past in our demure blue dresses and broad-brimmed hats, our eyes fixed on the path in front of us.

I started visiting the Sacred Heart Hospice in Darlinghurst on Saturdays as part of my gold Duke of Edinburgh award that Mrs Breen, my wonderful old English teacher in Inverell, had encouraged me to do. It was the late '80s, when the rates of infection from HIV were much higher in Australia than they are now and before antiretroviral drugs had transformed the treatment of HIV sufferers. The hospice was full of men in the last stages of full-blown AIDS, as well as those receiving palliative care for cancer and other terminal illnesses.

I hated seeing people so weak and wasted but I wasn't really shocked. I just used to go in and work out my priorities, how much time I had and what I could best do with it. It wasn't unlike going around with Mum in Inverell to see the old people in the nursing home. Mum would do physio with them, to rehabilitate them after strokes, and I'd sit with them and chat. And listen. That's really what these men wanted – to have a listener. Who or what that listener was probably didn't matter.

'G'day,' I'd say to one poor fella. 'I'm Gemma from St Vincent's. What's your name?'

'Greg,' he'd say.

'Where are you from, Greg? Got any brothers and sisters? Tell me a bit about them.'

And he'd unfold his life story over the next half hour.

We had a wonderful headmistress at St Vincent's, Sister Margie Byrne. She was quite progressive and as I was from a conservative religious background we clashed a few times, but only in a spirit of good humour. She didn't wear a habit, for example, which was unheard-of where I was from.

'Sister, I think you should go and put your habit on,' I said to her once as a joke. It was lovely and unusual to be able to have such friendly banter with your head teacher.

But despite those differences we became very good friends. In Year 12, I went to see her in her office.

'Sister Margie, I've been thinking a lot about what to do when I leave school,' I said. 'I want to go and work in Africa and I've been thinking about medicine but I'm also thinking about becoming a nun. What do you think?'

'Gemma,' she said, leaning forward and fixing me with a serious look. 'If you join the order, I'm *leaving* it!' She was only half joking.

Sister Margie explained that the first thing I needed to do was to go to university and get a useful qualification. Otherwise, if I went over to Africa without skills, I'd simply be taking a job from an unskilled local person, which would not help the situation. She went on to suggest, very gently, that perhaps I was not best suited to a life of obedience and patience, being – how could she put it? – a touch headstrong and overbearing about anything I set out to do. Also the Sisters of Charity – Sister Margie's order – didn't have any presence in Africa. But if I really wanted to explore the idea further she could put me in touch with the Sacred Heart order, which did a lot of work out in Africa.

Funnily enough, Father Ferdie, the Franciscan priest who used to visit us at home, had a niece who was working with the Sacred Heart order in Uganda. Through him, I later met Sister

Kay Hassler, a Sacred Heart nun who had been the head of a school in Uganda for many years but had come back to Australia for cancer treatment. She became a key figure in organising my first visit to Africa.

For the moment, I pushed longer-term plans to the back of my mind and redoubled my efforts to study for the Higher School Certificate. Maybe once a month I'd go out on a Saturday night, or on Sunday after church I'd go to a movie with the girls, but if I did that, I'd come back a bit earlier to make up for lost study time. I was able to go into my HSC exams and honestly say I could not have worked harder to achieve my goal of getting into medicine at Sydney or Melbourne universities.

And I didn't make it.

I missed out by 6 marks out of 500. I didn't even make it on the second round of offers. It was devastating. I cried for days. I'd never failed in anything before. I'd thought that if you set your mind to a goal and slogged away, you could achieve anything. But I discovered that sometimes, that's simply not enough.

For a while I didn't really care what I applied for instead. I could have applied to do medicine at a different university but I'd had my heart set on Sydney or Melbourne and I didn't want to accept anything less. Arrogance, I suppose. So I decided upon science at the University of Melbourne – Mum and Dad's old uni – with the thought that I could transfer across to medicine if my marks were good enough.

In the meantime, I was young, I had just got my P-plates and it was the Christmas holidays. After working so hard for so long, there was a lot of fun to be had. Dad lent me his four-wheel drive and my best school friend, Leasa, another mate Roseanne Kerlin and I headed for Dubbo and the first of a round of country parties. The next few years, *nominally*, would be given over to the study of science but I'd discovered my true forte: driving huge distances in thumping big cars to go to all-night B&S (Bachelor and Spinster) balls.

It would not be an exaggeration to say that in my whole university career I went to as few as 30 lectures in total, but I loved my life in college. I lived at Newman College, a co-ed Catholic college housed in a beautiful Walter Burley-Griffin building. I even stayed a year in exactly the same room as my own father had when he was at Newman. Dad had been passionate about Newman in his university days and would often tell me about the pranks that he and his mates would get up to – our shared passion for the college was another great bond between us.

There were ten of us at Newman studying science – though only one, Rebecca Harrison, was doing exactly my course – and we soon learned that if we pooled our efforts, we could all make it through with a minimum of effort. One of us had to attend each lecture, and then as exam time approached I would organise for all the lecture notes to be photocopied. As a group we would study together solidly for the two to three weeks leading up to the exams. It worked perfectly and freed up valuable time for going to B&Ss. Sometimes we'd drive two days to one Saturday night ball only to turn around, come back to Melbourne for a couple of days, and then head off again for the next Saturday's ball.

B&Ss had a culture of their own. I had a B&S calendar in my room, listing all the parties in all the towns for the year, and we tried to get to as many as we could. The only thing I'd make sure of was that I found somewhere to go to mass on Sunday morning. I remember one time, after driving for 20 straight hours from Melbourne to Armidale for Robb College's B&S, going to church with my brother Benn on the Sunday morning afterwards. Both of us were still covered in food dye from a water pistol fight the night before, we were probably pretty rank and my hair was disgusting. The two of us sat in the back row, trying to blend into the background, when I started hiccupping. That started Benn off laughing and, even though he would have been 23 or 24 to my 19, we both laughed ourselves stupid, like little kids.

The biggest attraction of the balls was meeting people. I've always found country people are really easygoing, laidback and blessed with a good sense of humour. At the time, I thought that city people were more artificial and pretentious. I was so obsessed with country life that if I'd walked into a pub, I wouldn't have considered talking to a boy unless he was wearing RM Williams, Red Wings or Thomas Cook boots, moleskin pants and a stripy shirt. It's funny – now I would not even look at what shoes someone was wearing. But all subcultures are like that – whether it's surfie, bikie, goth or country. They have their uniform and their rituals – and ours was staying up all night at a shed in a paddock somewhere in the outback, having drink fights and doing circle work in utes. When it was my twenty-first birthday party, Sarah Montague and Peta Credlin – two of my B&S mates – made their speech with one of the ball dresses I'd worn standing next to them. It was so full of rum and food dye that it could literally stand on its own. It was thanks to them that my parents found out about my double life and the exact number of lectures I had – or had not – attended while at university.

I didn't have the money for a car, so I'd bought myself a little Kawasaki 250 dirt bike to get to lectures and around town. I thought it was pretty great because I could avoid all the traffic and whiz up the main street in Melbourne, darting through the cars, riding down stairs and parking on the pavement, to buy some ball dress fabric or thread for a new B&S dress at Spotlight, the big craft shop.

A college friend of mine, Dan Malone, and I once decided on the spur of the moment to go to the Monash University ball. Dan grabbed his tux, I threw on a ballgown, we hopped on my bike and away we went. After dancing most of the night and crashing at the college there, we thought we'd head back to Newman, grabbing a bite to eat on the way. So, there we were, at the McDonald's drive-through, tired, dishevelled and filthy, but still wearing the full taffeta ballgown and black tie, on a dirt bike. Man, we had class. Dan had the room next to me and had such a good time at uni that he failed two years running. I got an email from him last year out of the blue. He did his doctorate in pharmacy and he's now Dr Dan Malone, lecturing at Melbourne University. Amazing.

Through going to B&Ss I'd met many new people. We became a family. Some of them were doing the same course as Rebecca and me but were from other colleges – some of them pretty wild and *definitely* not religious – and we all became great friends. Through the term, we'd go to parties together and share lecture notes. Then, two weeks before exam time, we'd become the night study group. At the end of each term, I'd organise my friends and give everyone a topic each. They'd have to go away and study it, then come back and teach the others what was important, with notes. Every evening we'd get together and study all through the night. We'd break for McDonald's at about 7.00 in the morning then go back to our rooms and collapse until the afternoon. In the evening, we'd begin the whole cycle again.

On one occasion, we were supposed to be studying for a genetics exam. I hadn't gone to a single lecture and was starting to panic.

'Guys,' I said to the group, 'I seriously don't understand a word of this. There is no way I can pass this exam.' Unfortunately, it seemed that we were all in the same desperate, hopeless boat. Then it occurred to me. If we were that desperate and hopeless, maybe we could call on the help of the patron saint of the desperate and hopeless himself: St Jude.

In the Catholic faith, there are saints for every situation. If you lose something, you call on St Anthony. If you're travelling, you ask for the help of St Christopher. Well, with St Anthony, I've never found a thing. With St Christopher, I still hit potholes. But St Jude? I'm increasingly sure that I have a direct line to that man and somehow I managed to convince this pack of seriously non-church-going party people that we needed the intervention of a saint to help us through the exams. They probably thought I was mad but they were desperate and just worried enough to give it a go.

When you really need a saint's help, you can say a prayer – or, rather, a series of prayers – called a novena. If you say your novena for nine days in a row, it can be granted. If you're really, really desperate, you can do it every hour for nine hours instead. We were really, really desperate. So the night before the exams, we were up all night studying and every hour on the hour we'd take a quick break. I'd read out a prayer to St Jude – from the back of a St Jude's prayer card – and they'd all repeat it back to me. After each prayer, we then had to do one Our Father, one Hail Mary and one Glory Be. They were okay on the Our Father – *just* – but I had to lead them through the Hail Marys and Glory Bes line by line. But we all passed, that time and every time afterwards.

The only exception was when one of our group, Sarah, had to repeat a subject for some bizarre reason. A year later, she was still at uni and I was away in the Northern Territory doing my honours year. I got a phone call from Sarah, an ex-Geelong Grammar girl and as wild and non-religious as they come.

'Hey, Gem. How does that novena to St Jude go again? I'm getting desperate.'

I talked her through the prayers. She thanked me and rang off. I later heard that she'd breezed through. I don't think Sarah's ever been to church again, though, so I can't really claim a lasting conversion, but a few months ago I had an email from her. After ten years, she still carries the St Jude's prayer in her wallet!

Ever since I went down to Sydney to boarding school, I'd been moving away from horses and serious riding. When I was away from home I couldn't exercise my horses so for a while Dad would do it for me and bring them down for me to ride in Sydney. I didn't go so well though, and Dad would shake his head sadly and say: 'I'm sorry, Gem, but you've lost your saddle bum.' I missed riding terribly but it's not something to which you can only give intermittent attention: it's got to be all or nothing. At least, with me it does.

So when a very different riding challenge arose at uni, I was more than ready for it – camel-racing. One of my friends at college, Anna O'Sullivan, was the eldest of nine children, from Patchewollock in the Mallee in northern Victoria. The O'Sullivans lived at a property that backed onto a desert, complete with moving sand dunes, and they were great people. Tim O'Sullivan, Anna's dad, used to raise money for the Flying Doctors by organising an annual camel race – Mud to the Dust – from the Otways on the Great Ocean Road to Patchewollock, a distance of 660 kilometres. He'd round up some wild camels from the desert and they'd use this long endurance race to break them in, fundraising all the way. Tim had heard I'd been a bit of a rider and wondered whether I'd like to try something new: would I like to join the race? You bet I would.

The camel I was given to ride was a young blonde girl, called Ballerina because of her long legs. I wasn't fooled by her sweet name and doe eyes. She was one wild child. She'd been caught four months before and was a vicious biter. I used to have to hobble her when she sat down so she couldn't get back up. Unlike horses, camels are 'automatic leaders': that is, if they have a nose peg and a rope on, they'll let themselves be led. They don't like the sensation of having their nose peg pulled so the lightest tug on the reins should stop them.

There were five or six camels in the race, as well as 20 or so horses and support people in cars and on foot, making our way up the highway. The horses would cover more ground than us during the day, but at night we'd pass them sleeping beside the road. Our camels didn't need as much sleep and could walk all day and night. We'd stop every 30 kilometres or so when we physically could not sit for a moment longer. The back-up team would cook us some food and the camels would grab some grass, then we'd swing our screaming legs back into the saddle and go again. Every few days we'd have a rest day and sleep like the dead.

I started the race and Ballerina was doing well. I was riding her like a horse and she trotted along obediently. Then, all of a sudden, a car came along. Ballerina, being a wild desert flower, didn't know about cars and her first impressions weren't favourable. Before I could do anything, she'd pivoted on her back legs and started galloping flat chat in the wrong direction. It felt like we backtracked hundreds of kilometres, with me pulling on her nose peg and yelling at her. Eventually, as the Otways came back into view, I pulled so hard the nose peg ripped out. There was blood everywhere. I felt terrible, but at least we stopped and could regroup and turn ourselves around.

After that, Ballerina was much more docile and less spooked by cars and we rejoined the others. But days later, towards the end of the race, as we drew into Castlemaine one evening, I noticed that she was tiring. Where we'd been running, now we walked. Ballerina and I had bonded by this time – apart from the occasional chomp – and it was very peaceful walking along the road at night, just the two of us, under a star-sprinkled sky.

Camels are absolutely silent and I had brought a harmonica, which I played very badly, so we moseyed along to the wheeze of my mouth organ. Then Ballerina sat down. And wouldn't get up. Tim O'Sullivan looked back and saw I was having difficulties so he turned around and came to my aid.

'You've got to let her know who's boss, Gem,' he said. 'Get your whip out, 'cause if you let her sit down, she'll get into bad habits for life.' Farmers aren't very sentimental about animals.

I pulled out a stirrup leather and tried to give her a whack. Ballerina didn't get up but she did swivel round so that her bum was out of my reach. I tried again: arm raise, swivel swivel. I managed to connect a couple of times but without much result. She was one clever camel.

'You go on,' I said to Tim. 'I'll catch up with you at Castlemaine.' After a bit of a rest, we did make it to Castlemaine at 3.00 in the morning. They'd kept the pub open and the locals were out in force to see the camels, which were allowed right inside the pub, next to the pool tables. Everyone from the race had stayed up to see me and Ballerina in safely and it was a great night, with a wonderful family spirit.

Two days later, we restarted the race. Normally, when you restart, everyone goes hell for leather for the first two kilometres out of town, to please the crowd and so raise more money for the Flying Doctors, for whom the race was in aid. We usually started at a gallop or even a trot but Ballerina refused. She started at a walk and slowed to an amble.

We soon dropped behind. I hopped off and we walked along together. She needed to rest but I didn't want to quit the race. Every now and then she'd stop for some grass but she'd always come back to me, which was lovely. I was walking up behind her when suddenly I noticed that there was a bag protruding from under her tail.

'She's having a baby!' I yelled. An old man passing in his white ute stopped to see what was wrong and offered his help. Another passing guy lent me his UHF radio so that I could call ahead and speak to Charlie Cornell, one of the back-up crew and an experienced camel-handler.

'Gemma,' said Charlie, 'I know camels, and that camel is not having a baby. Not today at any rate – she's nowhere near big enough. Maybe in four months' time. If anything's happening now, then it must be a miscarriage.'

I just burst into tears. Poor Ballerina had been pregnant and all I could do was hit her and push her and try to show her who was boss and now she'd miscarried, all because of me. I pulled her to the side of the road and made her lie down on my saddle blanket, patting her and telling her how sorry I was. I was still sobbing when Ballerina started to rock on her knees and groan. She was swaying to the right, then the left, then suddenly a head popped out from between her legs. And it moved. I quickly got back on the UHF to Charlie, who was still fifteen minutes away.

'Charlie, I have no idea about camels but I do know with lambs and calves that their legs are supposed to come out before their head. Is it the same with camels?'

'Yep, the legs should come out first, Gemma,' Charlie said. 'They're really long. You'll have to go in and find them carefully to pull out the calf.'

So the old farmer from the ute and I washed our hands and went in and somehow managed to untangle the calf's endless legs and pull him out. He was a baby boy, jet black, the cutest thing you ever saw. I called him Basil, after my dad, and because we were just outside the little town of Boort he became Basil from Boort. I actually had done it all wrong as camels are supposed to have their calves standing up rather than sitting down. When the calf falls onto the ground, the bump is supposed to knock it into life – a bit like hitting a human baby on the tail at birth – but it didn't seem to matter to young Basil.

Because the whole thing had been broadcast over the UHF radio, within half an hour everyone from the race was there. Within three-quarters of an hour, a television crew had arrived. Everyone loves a baby camel.

At the end of each leg of the race we had a trophy-giving ceremony, for the fastest time, most improved and that sort of thing. At the end of this leg, I was solemnly presented with a card: *Congratulations on your new baby boy* with messages inside saying things like, *Didn't we warn you that humping at night creates babies?*

The O'Sullivans told me they were going to give me Basil for my twenty-first. I was thrilled, not least because Dad's favourite old horse, Dion, had died and I had visions of him mustering sheep on Basil. But sadly, a couple of days before they were due to bring him up, Basil broke his leg and had to be put down. About a year later, Tim developed a brain tumour and died really quickly. The camel races petered out, because he'd been the driving force behind them. He was the most beautiful man who led the most wonderful family.

The camel race was one of the greatest experiences of those university years but now I was nearing the end and had to work out what to do next. Throughout university I'd kept in touch with Kay Hassler, the Sister who'd worked with the Sacred Heart order in Uganda. She'd been headmistress of a school in Uganda but had had to return to Melbourne when she became ill with cancer. Sister Kay showed me pictures of the school there, outside a town called Masaka, and told me she could arrange for me to work there when I graduated if I added on a Diploma of Education.

She was wonderfully forthright about what I could expect: 'Africa's hard. Don't expect it to be romantic. I promise you the thrill will wear off pretty quickly when there's no electricity or running water and you're sick to death of eating the same food. Too many people go there with unrealistic expectations. They don't last very long.'

Even with those words of caution, the Sister's passion for Africa was obvious and contagious, as was her belief that education was the way forward for the constantly troubled continent. In a way, separated though we were by age and experience, we were also soul mates.

Despite the B&Ss and nice country boyfriends with big utes – basically, your average selfish late teens/early twenties lifestyle – I'd always kept up some voluntary work. I'd started to expand the community service program at Newman College, organising students who wanted to become involved in things like Alcoholics Anonymous, mentoring children or feeding homeless people. Everyone was really into it, which was great. I was still interested in exploring a religious life and, aside from that, I knew I still wanted to go to Africa. First, though, I needed to follow my parents' and my former headmistress's advice and gain some proper qualifications.

After graduating with a very indifferent Bachelor's degree in science, I talked my way into the honours program at the University of the Northern Territory, by promising my supervisor a lot of hard work and a trip to the Birdsville races if he took me on. He gave in, but declined the trip to Birdsville.

During my final year at university, I'd majored in genetics and biochemistry and found it really interesting as well as feeling that the information might be useful if I ended up on the land. So my area of research for the honours year was studying and manipulating the wheat genome, in the hope that it might lead to a new, more drought-resistant strand of wheat being developed. Even though I would receive a First-Class Honours degree, I knew down deep that I had no intention of pursuing science as my career.

I decided to drive up to Darwin from home. By this stage, Dad had found out about my dirt bike and insisted that I drive a car, which he helped me buy. It was a great big fuel-guzzling steel monster of a Valiant. You could not even see the colour of its big boot for the B&S stickers and slogans plastered over it.

'I know it's old, Gemma,' said Dad. 'But if you have an accident with another car, this one's going to come out on top.'

Dad helped me load the car for the trip. He filled up a few jerry cans with water and another three with petrol and slung them in the boot. Then he pulled out a .22 and handed it to me. At the time, there had been stories about people in the outback who'd stopped to help someone lying in the road and then been ambushed. Dad's little girl was taking off for a big four-day trip by herself up to the Territory and he wasn't taking any chances.

'Keep it near you at all times,' he said. 'If anyone's lying in the road in front of you, drive straight over them. If you need to use the gun, don't hesitate.' I never used it, but it stayed under a blanket on my back seat for the next few months.

It was a great year in Darwin. I worked with two girls who were also in the honours program: Cathy Eupene, who was working in the same area as I was, under the same supervisor, and Carrie Michell, who was from a completely wild family in Katherine. Carrie and her elder sister rode bulls, which I'd never seen a woman do – if you didn't count my attempt with Gus. Carrie was also one of the most impressive drinkers I've ever known, with one of the biggest hearts as well. I was terribly sad a couple of years ago when I received an email telling me that she'd died. She left a real legacy – there's even some new species of plants in the Northern Territory that were named after her, as she had done a lot for the national parks there. Carrie, Cathy and I did everything together. We were like a set of triplets and when it was hot and we weren't in the lab, we would fill up a plastic baby pool and wallow in about two cups of water.

After honours, I returned home to do my Dip Ed at Armidale. I'd wanted a year at home with Mum and Dad and needed to start saving money for Africa. Things had changed at Wyoming. In 1991, the government had removed the base wool price and the value of our stock plummeted. At Christmas time, when usually we'd sell close to 10,000 lambs, we sold nothing. We didn't even have enough feed for them, so Dad tried to give them to the abattoir, but everyone else was trying to do the same thing. Even the abattoir wouldn't take them. Finally, the farmers were offered $1.20 for each sheep they shot – sheep that had been worth $70 or $80. Dad had to shoot thousands of animals and it broke his heart. He lost faith in the government and in farming, but – and this is the mark of the man – never in himself. Instead of giving up, he dusted himself off and went back into the legal profession. He had kept up with all the yearly conferences over the years he worked with the sheep, but it was still a big step for him. Ten years later, he had offices in Armidale and Tamworth. My dear brother Benn stepped in to keep the property going as, despite the hardship, no one in the family wanted to sell it; we will always be indebted to him. Over the following years it was Benn who gradually got Dad back into the woolshed – he really was a very special sheep farmer with a gift for classing wool.

However, in this year that I stayed at home to do my diploma, Dad was busy in his law office and Benn was down in Ballarat earning better money than he could make on the land. With my youngest brothers still away at school, I was able to help out on the property and do my bit for the family. While we'd lost some sheep, we still had a fair few to look after. I also had a scheme for raising some money for Africa, buying up cheap calves – a by-product of the dairy industry – and bringing them up at Wyoming for eventual sale.

Being a city girl, Mum was invaluable in ensuring the smooth running of the homestead, but her main work was in the house and not the yard. Yet she always rose to the occasion when she was needed. Because Mum had trained as a physiotherapist, she had a sound background in basic medicine and was always being asked to patch up animals and people, friends and strangers, who had come to grief in and around our property, especially on the gravel road which ran outside our front gate. There was one horrific accident where some boys rolled their car on the rough road. One of them came running to our house, shocked and panting.

'There's been an accident!'

Mum, as always, calmly took charge. 'Right. Is anyone bleeding?'

'My mate. It's his arm. He was sleeping in the back and I think his arm must have been hanging out the window.'

Mum gathered her first aid kit and raced down to the site of the accident. The poor boy's arm was hanging uselessly, nearly severed, and there was a lot of blood. Coolly, Mum did what she could and bandaged the boy up before taking him into town to hospital, a good hour away. He was told by his doctors that without her help he would almost certainly have lost his life. A few months after he got out of hospital he drove all the way out to Wyoming to thank Mum personally.

So Mum was always good in a crisis and that year when I was, in effect, in charge of the day-to-day running of the property, we definitely had a crisis. It was drought, of course, as it so often is. This time, it was so dry and there was so little feed that when the ewes lambed, they were too weak and sick to look after their babies. The lambs were in danger of starvation – if the foxes didn't get them first. But the sheep still needed drenching – dosing with liquid medicine – and shearing so I had to muster them up to the stockyards on my own – a huge job. We still had over 1000 sheep to bring in from one of the paddocks, and I really needed Mum's help, even though she never normally came to muster. As always, when you really needed her, Mum was there.

Usually we'd muster on horseback or motorbike but that year the sheep were walking so slowly and there were so many motherless lambs that we had to do most of it on foot. As well as mustering, Mum and I organised all the shearing and crutching – trimming the face and rear – of sheep together just to keep the property while Benn and Dad earned money in other ways. Eventually I brought one of my horses down to help out. Mum picked up the lambs that were too weak to walk and straddled them over the back of the horse until she had rescued probably fifteen. It was a beautiful sight to see Mum coming over the ridge, leading my horse, which was piled with little lambs. She mightn't have been bred a country girl but, my goodness, at that moment she exemplified country resourcefulness and grit. Sadly many of those lambs were true orphans – not like the ones I had boldly taken years before when I was a young girl and had to give to old man Stumpy.

Even though it was very hard work I loved being home for that year. I helped out with Mum and Dad and completed my Dip Ed. But my focus was really on Africa now, not my studies. The one-year post-grad course seemed overly theoretical and unrelated to my experiences. For me, the best things were the 'pracs' where you went out into the field and actually taught. My first was at a high school across on the coast from New England and man, it was wild. The kids were spitting on the stairs, there seemed to be no discipline and I was glad to get out of there.

Then I went to a local Catholic school, St Joseph's, and at the end of it was offered a paid job, which was how I raised some of the money to go to Africa in addition to selling calves. Teaching came naturally to me. The public speaking and drama and debating had made me confident in front of an audience, which helped because if you show fear, the children can be merciless. Mum had always said I'd be a good teacher and perhaps it was true. I wasn't necessarily the sort of teacher who'd inspire you with a lifelong love of learning, but more the sort you could trust to get you through exams. Sometimes that's the most useful person you can have at the front of your classroom.

My Dip Ed, much like my science degree, was simply a ticket, a functional ticket to enable me to go to Africa. My dream had never left me but I was unsure of the path my future would take. Maybe in Africa I would discover that my true vocation was to become a nun. Then again, maybe I'd come back and marry a nice farmer with a V8 ute, have six children and do a bit of casual teaching on the side.

With Sister Kay Hassler's help, I was able to have my plane ticket paid for by Palms, a charity that organises volunteer placements around the world. Sister Kay had already arranged for me to work and live at Kalungu Girls' Training Centre just outside Masaka in Uganda.

I'd only once left Australia and that was on a very organised, week-long, first-world tour with a Catholic youth group. This time I was leaving on my own, for at least two years, to go and live and work in a developing country. As I said goodbye to Mum and Dad through my tears, I had a brief moment of doubt.

'Well, Gemma, no one's making you go,' said Mum. 'You're the one who wants to.'

'I know,' I said, holding Dad's hand tighter, tears streaming down my face. 'I'm just having a moment, that's all.'

I suppose I was sad too of course, and a little nervous. But above all else, I really was excited at last to be embarking upon something that could test my desire for adventure and challenge in a bigger arena than I'd ever encountered. I felt like I'd been in training for a long time – now I was going to see some action.

CHAPTER THREE

I've probably flown from Australia to Africa and back well over 20 times now but that first trip to Uganda is still etched sharply in my mind. Everything was a first for me, every experience startlingly new.

I flew into Harare Airport in Zimbabwe and was amazed by the sea of black people. (What else I'd been expecting, I don't know.) The air even seemed different, hot and dusty and full of the smell of warm bodies. I took a shuttle bus to an overnight hotel and had my first tussle with a porter for my bags. I'd always humped my own bags around and had never expected to receive *service*. Later I would discover that in Africa, there are so many people and so few jobs going around that to deny someone the chance to help you does them a disservice, as well as being considered rude.

From Zimbabwe I flew to Nairobi, Kenya, to meet my plane to Uganda. As I sat with a book unopened on my lap, in a travel-induced limbo, I saw a familiar-looking white face amidst the crowd.

'Gemma, is that you?' he said, coming up to give me a hug. It was an old Newman College friend of mine, Ed Poliness, who'd studied medicine in the year above me and was on his way back home after completing a three-month internship in Kenya. When he discovered that it was actually me and that it was my first-ever trip to Africa, he gave me just one piece of advice.

'If you get into any sort of trouble, hand over some money. Everyone's bribeable here. Even if they're throwing the book at you for some infringement or other, it's just for show. Remember that when you get into a spot of bother.'

His words were not exactly inspiring, but they were practical and, in time, they've stood me in pretty good stead.

But, as I was to learn, while there might be corruption at every level in everyday African life, there is also a completely different level of courtesy and charm, two examples of which I experienced even on that first flight from Nairobi to Uganda. One was embodied in a beautiful African lady who was sitting across the aisle from me. Now that I've lived in Africa for so long, I probably wouldn't give her a second glance. Back then, I could not drag my eyes from her. I had never seen anyone with more natural elegance. She was dressed incredibly vibrantly, with an intricately wrapped turban, and she had the deep, velvety black skin of the Ugandans that sets off colourful fabrics so well. I knew that I was staring and didn't want her to think me rude but at the same time I was fascinated. I kept pretending to rummage in the overhead locker so that I could look down and sneak another glance. She glanced up and smiled warmly at me. It was a brief moment but it set the tone for so many people I would meet over the next few years. I don't know how they do it but Africans, especially the women, carry themselves so beautifully and wear clothes with such style. Even the poorest people look groomed and proud. They might only have one pair of shoes but that pair will be gleaming. We're such riffraff by comparison.

But African manners go much further than superficial grace. Shopkeepers will always greet you politely and ask how you are, and strangers will try to welcome you into their homes. There is so much generosity from people who have so little that when I first arrived in Africa, I was defensive, thinking that everyone wanted something from me. In truth, some of them did, but not all, and the politeness and courtesy remain the same whether someone is trying to look after you or rip you off. In fact, even the people who have cheated you still greet you like their long-lost friend. It doesn't make up for the initial fraud or betrayal, but it does make life a lot more pleasant and friendly.

My other experience on the plane was with a lovely Ugandan man who invited me to stay with him and his family. I explained that I was being picked up by Sister Margie, a Canadian nun who was the head of the Sacred Heart Sisters, but thanked him all the same. However, when we arrived at Entebbe Airport that evening, there was no one waiting to collect me. My new, fatherly friend insisted on staying with me until he knew I was safe and, after several days of travel, feeling a long way from home, I was very happy to let him. Just as night fell and I was ready to give up and go back with him to his family, two nuns came running down the road and flying into Arrivals: Sister Margie and a Spanish nun in her eighties, Sister Paulina.

'Are you Gemma?' The elderly women were breathless. I nodded. 'I'm so sorry, our car's broken down. We've had to run around and find another car.'

Welcome to Africa, I thought, and followed them out into the night and onwards to their convent in Kampala.

The next day, I packed my things into an old Canter truck, a rickety little machine, jacked up about four feet off the ground, and headed off to my new life with the Sisters in Kalungu, where I would spend the next few years.

Even though I was to teach at the school, I lived at the convent, with the Sisters. However, I had my own room and wasn't expected to participate fully in their life of devotion. I did most of the time anyway as I enjoyed it and it was invaluable for me to experience convent life up close. Invaluable, because after years of thinking about becoming a nun, it took only two or three months for me to realise that it wasn't the life for me. It wasn't anything in particular but I realised that nuns didn't become different people when they donned the habit. They were just ordinary human beings trying to do the best they could for what they believed in. They chose their vocation and not whom to live with, so they had to make a lot of personal sacrifices. And human beings, especially a group of women living together, could have problems with each other. The sisters were very tolerant of me but I just wanted to get out there and meet the people, learn the language and do what needed to be done.

I realised that, while there were some fantastic religious organisations in Africa and some really experienced men and women in them who are just wisdom personified, there were also a lot of people doing good work in Africa who weren't wearing habits.

At Kalungu Girls' Training Centre, I loved my students and my fellow teachers. Initially I was employed to teach science and maths, but pretty early on in my stay I discovered a pile of disused old pedal sewing machines in the shed where the school stored the corn, which the girls themselves grew, harvested and cooked. We were a little way out of Kalungu town – about a five-minute walk to the town centre, which was a cluster of ten little tin-shack shops. So the school was surrounded by lush, green small holdings where farmers scratched out a modest subsistence.

I've always loved sewing and made money all through uni sewing party dresses for friends. It seems to me that sewing is a very useful, portable skill to have, especially somewhere like Africa. If you need to make money, if your husband leaves you or the crops fail, you can always sew. Even if you're studying to be a doctor, you need to have skills to earn money to keep yourself fed while you're in college. So I started a sewing class for the girls and it became so popular that after a while I dropped my maths and science classes and they brought in an extra teacher for those subjects so that I could concentrate on sewing.

As were most of the schools run by religious orders in Uganda, Kalungu Girls' was a private, fee-based institution, catering to the children of the middle classes. Kalungu wasn't as expensive as some – and by Western standards, the fees were very low – but it was out of the reach of many of the ordinary local people. Most of the 400-odd students came from Masaka – 30 minutes' drive away – or the capital, Kampala.

My best local friend, Gertrude, the art teacher, for instance, had a very clever little sister, Winnie, whose family could not afford to send her to a school like Kalungu initially, although they would have loved to. Winnie was about sixteen years old and feisty with it. We were always helping her to get out of sticky situations – she definitely had initiative. But even though the school we worked in was relatively elite, being so close to a struggling small town we also saw a very different side of African life, where poor, overcrowded home conditions were the norm and where most children would be lucky to be educated after the age of eight or nine.

It was something we often talked about, Gertrude and I – how to break the cycle of poverty for these children and, closer to home, how to help her little sister get ahead. Without English, computer skills, decent maths, science or any trades, no matter how bright they were, these children were not being educated for anything more than a life on the farm or in petty crime. I promised that one day, when I was back in Australia and earning Western money, I would lend a hand in funding Winnie's education, even helping her to start university, because I really believed that she had the brains and the spirit to do something with her life.

I also started thinking longer term, about how to make the most difference to the greatest number of people in Africa and the answer, for me, always came back to education. It seemed to me that no matter how much money well-meaning foreign organisations poured into Africa, without raising the basic standards of education across the board, it was like filling a leaky bucket. The uneducated would always remain under the power of the educated, inequalities between them would always lead to abuse, and corruption would always be rife. And the situation would worsen with every successive generation. But if money was directed toward education, then ordinary Africans could grow up expecting to earn a living and competently run their own services, and each generation of schoolchildren would have a chance of creating a fairer society. Fighting poverty through education. I liked the sound of that. At the back of my mind, I even began to formulate a fantasy plan about building my own school in Uganda.

But these thoughts were vague and for the future. For the moment, I was 23, living in Africa and having the time of my life. Africa was a real adventure and the Sisters let me have as much freedom as possible, within reason. Sometimes Gertrude would come with me when I had to drive the school truck into Masaka town for supplies and we would go to the local bars and restaurants, or we'd hang out with the other teachers outside the staff room, gossiping for hours. It was so easy to meet people and form real friendships with them. I'm sure part of my attraction for the others was novelty. Kalungu was a very isolated rural village and the closest big town, Masaka, with a population of more than 60,000, having been flattened by the Tanzanian Army when they ousted Idi Amin in 1979, was still far from being a tourist destination. The closest Westerner in age to me was Sister Anne and she was in her sixties. So even the other adult teachers were fascinated by me, by my pale skin and long brown hair, and the children were constantly touching me, playing with my hair, stroking my arms.

Only one other young Westerner came to the school and that was later in my stay. Kathy Glaser was an American girl with a Ugandan mother who'd come out to experience her mother's country. She was great fun and together we decided to visit the gorillas in the Impenetrable Forest a national park of some 300-odd square kilometres that was one of the last remaining habitats of the mountain gorilla. Tours to see the gorillas were very expensive, especially for two girls on non-Western salaries, so we decided to hitchhike there and back. A priest from a nearby seminary gave us a lift to Kabale but we then needed transport to take us on the four-hour trip to the Impenetrable Forest. We asked around the town if anyone could lend us a bike and finally found someone with a little Suzuki 100: a young bloke who was happy to rent it out for $20 as long as we had it back by the following evening.

We must have looked a sight on that bike. Kathy and I are both big girls and that little bike, with us squeezed on top, probably did a top speed of 20 kilometres per hour. I only wore skirts in Uganda out of respect for the Sisters and because, it being a rural area, you never saw women in pants. But on the bike we couldn't wear skirts so we stuck on our pyjamas and away we went on the rough dirt road, the bike whining in protest. Nyyyyyeeeeeee. By the time we got to the forest, the four-hour trip had turned into an eight-hour trip. We were so exhausted, we couldn't even eat dinner.

But we found the gorillas at last. The day before they'd raided a farm in the forest and been chased away by farmers brandishing sticks, so they were even shyer than usual and had hidden away on the other side of the forest. It's not called 'impenetrable' for nothing. You could hold your hand out in front of your face and lose it in the trees. A couple of guards with big machetes accompanied us. They just hacked through the vines and we followed. At the end, we had a beautiful hour with the gorillas. From our camouflaged vantage point, hidden by thick vegetation, we watched a family group going about their daily business. Seeing the expression on a mother gorilla's face as she nursed her infant underlined how much we share with these gentle apes. Both Kathy and I felt touched by magic to see them up close. Then we hopped on our little bike and headed back for Kabale, mosquitoes splatting in our faces as we rode through the dark – which was when we discovered the bike had no headlights – to make sure we got it back to its owner before our deadline.

I had many great trips but none of them was more memorable – or had more far-reaching consequences – than my first visit to Tanzania.

I'd arrived in Uganda in January 1995 for the start of the school year and had immediately immersed myself in my work. I had brought over walking boots, backpacks and travel guides in the hope that I'd do some travelling but I put them all away and concentrated on settling in and getting to know the girls and my immediate area. By Easter, I was looking forward to exploring further afield. I'd met a lovely young English girl called Claire

Knighton, who worked at a boys' secondary school in a village not far from where I was working. Both of us wanted to go on a safari and we decided we'd travel together to Tanzania during the Easter holidays to see the Serengeti plains.

It was a great trip. We were on the shoestring of all shoestrings and neither of us could have cared less. I don't think we even noticed it. It's funny how it works that way. When you don't have any luxuries in your life it's not an issue, but the moment you do have them, you get used to them and can't imagine how you survived before. First we had a few nights in Kenya in $1.50-a-night fleapits – no sheets, broken roofs, pretty filthy – then we caught the Arusha Express to Tanzania. *Express?* Hah!! A journey that now takes five hours took all day. The bus stopped at every Maasai village between Nairobi and Arusha for villagers to get on and off, with their chickens and goats. Children weed on the floor. By the time we arrived in Arusha, the bus smelled completely feral.

But it was my first African travelling experience and I loved it. I loved looking out the window at the wild Maasai lands, over-grazed by their pampered cattle, dotted with spiny umbrella acacias, which to me symbolise Africa more than any other tree. Every so often, the dusty brown landscape would be splashed with colour and you'd see the Maasai themselves by the side of the road, the men in their gorgeous red and blue blankets tending their animals or the women, heavily laden with intricately beaded jewellery, carrying baskets to the market.

As we gradually climbed to Arusha, the landscape changed. Camel-coloured dust gave way to rich chocolate earth and suddenly the roads were lined with banana palms, coffee bushes and scarlet bougainvillea. The air – outside the bus, that is – felt clearer, higher, and we could see the peak of Mount Meru hovering in the clouds above the town. I had a brief impression of a place that felt tropical and fertile, then the bus pulled in at the bus station and I was, literally, clawed back to reality by the outstretched hands thrusting themselves into the bus, holding business cards for local safari companies.

'You want safari?'

'Here, here, for cheap safaris.'

'You want climb Kilimanjaro?'

'Good, clean rooms, very cheap.'

Arusha is the safari Mecca of Tanzania, being the jump-off point for tours to the Serengeti, Lake Manyara and the Ngorongoro Crater. It's also where thousands of tourists start their climb of Mount Kilimanjaro, Africa's highest mountain. So the people of Arusha are dependent on the safari and climbing business. April, when we arrived, is the quietest time of the year for tour operators because of the rains, and the 'flycatchers' – the touts whose job it is to pull in the tourists – were desperate.

We got off the bus clutching six or seven cards and then were faced with half a dozen or so men saying, 'You took my card, now you have to come to my office to talk about safari.'

'Not right now, thanks,' I said. 'We're really tired and we're just going to find our backpackers' and sleep.'

Turning our backs on the clamour of the bus station, we pulled out our brand new, hardly touched *Lonely Planet*s and started walking up Stadium Road to find the Micheli guesthouse. As we trudged along, lugging our backpacks, a Land Rover slowed down and purred beside us, with three boys inside. A very cocky bloke – I vaguely recognised him as one of the flycatchers – leaned out of the car.

'Hey girls, do you want a lift? We're going to Micheli's. I'm Andy and this is Mike and he' – gesturing inside to the driver hidden in the dark – 'is Richard.'

'No, thank you,' Claire said firmly. It was hot and late and we were filthy and tired, but we were not going to get in a car with a bunch of strange men. The boys continued on, driving beside us at walking pace, chatting us up, until they realised that we weren't going to be swayed, and hooned off.

About one hour later, we finally arrived, exhausted and sweaty, at our hostel and plonked our backpacks down in the dingy lounge, only to find Andy and Mike already comfortably in residence, sitting back with a couple of cold beers. 'I told you you should have had a lift, girls,' said Andy, smirking.

We ignored them and went in to clean up with a cold bucket shower. When we came back, they were still there so we asked them if they knew a good local chicken and rice joint. We weren't interested in over-priced Western food. They took us to a great little restaurant where we had a beautiful dinner for 60 cents. By this time, we'd relaxed and realised that Andy and Mike were great guys, complete motormouths and very funny. Their friend Richard had joined us but he didn't add much to the conversation. He made one comment in halting English to which I exclaimed: 'Oh my God, the boy talks!' And he subsided back into silence. By the end of the evening, we'd booked a five-day safari with Andy and Mike through Paradise Safaris.

The next morning we went to the office of their safari company and Richard came in, wearing black Levis and a dark denim workshirt. He was a strongly muscled bloke, with an air of authority even though he was only in his late twenties. I kicked Claire under the table.

'He's a bit okay, don't you think?' I whispered at her. She rolled her eyeballs.

'Admire, but don't touch,' she said.

Andy approached us. 'Listen, girls, there's been a change of plans. I've got to wait in town for some Irish boys who are going to come on the safari with us halfway through. Richard here will take you instead of me.'

'No worries,' we said. It was all the same to us: strong, silent type or motormouths; we just wanted to go and see some animals. We set off in one of Paradise Safaris' black-and-white zebra-striped Land Rovers: me, Claire, Iddi (the cook), Richard and a bearded Canadian who was so silent he may as well not have been there. Not Claire and I, though. As we drove out of Arusha and through the dust storms of the Maasai plains, we kept up a barrage of questions and comments for the taciturn Richard. He probably wished he'd brought ear plugs.

'Where are you from, Richard?'

'Where are your family?'

'How many brothers and sisters do you have?'

'What's that lake over there?'

'What's that tree called?'

And so on, and on.

Poor Richard's English most certainly was not up to two excitable girls who wanted a chat. But boy, he did know what he was doing, both behind the wheel and on safari. It was uncanny how he could spot the head of a sleeping lion from half a kilometre away or know exactly where which animals would be at any given time of the day. I came to respect him, watching him at work in his element, but I certainly didn't think of him outside his role as our safari driver.

Once we reached the Rift Valley, the dust subsided and we began to see the wild, untouched country unfolding in front of us. On our first day at Lake Manyara, we stopped the car to have lunch in the shade of an umbrella acacia, looking out over the lake. The cook set up our lunch and the setting was magical, with a group of hippos wallowing quite close to us and the lake hazed with a pink glow from millions of flamingos. I couldn't believe how much wildlife we'd already seen. There were monkeys in the trees and just that morning we'd rounded a corner and seen baboons sitting by the roadside, calmly scratching themselves and ignoring us. I had to keep reminding myself that we weren't in some amazing fenceless zoo but in the African bush, that these animals were here not for us but because it was their home, as it had been for millennia.

I walked over to the Land Rover to grab my camera. I'd already shot a full roll of film in one morning – a lot of zebra camouflaged by shadows – but I wanted to see if I could capture the flamingos on the lake. As I reached into the back of the car, I suddenly realised that Richard had followed me. Before I knew what was happening, he was behind me and had wrapped his arms around me. I acted instinctively, with a quick elbow to his unsuspecting, unbraced stomach. Boof! Richard reeled away, bent over, clutching himself.

I turned around and glared at him.

'How dare you? That is *so* unprofessional. We're your clients – how dare you make a move on me!'

I was genuinely appalled. I knew that Claire and I had been friendly and chatty but that wasn't a green light that we were available. I didn't know whether he thought all Western women were easy or had misread some connection between us but, whatever his thoughts, his actions were out of line and seriously unwelcome.

I had to admit that I had briefly thought about how handsome he was, but it had been just admiring him from a distance, because of his physical characteristics, the way you do with a stranger in the street. I'd certainly never contemplated anything actually happening with him.

Once he'd regained his breath, Richard apologised in a muffled voice. But he wouldn't meet my eyes. He didn't explain his extraordinary behaviour and went back to silent mode, which made the whole incident seem bizarrely unrelated to the rest of our trip, as if I'd imagined it. But I was very pleased not to have to talk to him for a few days. Of course, I told Claire about his behaviour and we both agreed that it was shocking. What a sleazebag. He probably had a girl on every safari. There was no way either of us could ever have anything to do with someone like that. Except there was still a little voice at the back of my mind whispering that he *was* cute to look at.

The safari moved on towards the Ngorongoro Crater and the incredible wildlife dispelled all thoughts of Richard's strange behaviour. The thrill of seeing animals in the wild never lessens for me. It's as exciting for me today as it was on that first safari. And I couldn't get over the magnificent trees – the beautiful flat-topped acacias, the ancient, swollen baobabs. Richard took us to see one baobab that was so enormous that you could park the car right inside its trunk. Apparently it was used as a hiding spot for poachers in the old days. Sadly, poaching is still a major problem in East Africa, despite changes to the laws in ivory trading. There will always be poor villagers who are prepared to risk their lives to make hundreds of times their annual salary for one elephant tusk or rhino horn.

By this time we'd been joined by Andy and Mike and two hilarious Irish boys. At Karatu, a nondescript town outside the crater, we went to a big tourist dinner, with fantastic acrobats to entertain us. I had one beer and then another. Only a couple, but enough to make me feel a bit relaxed when I realised Richard was standing beside me at the bar, looking wary but hopeful. I smiled and we began to talk; Richard started to look happier and more comfortable than he had in days. He still made sure he kept a very professional distance between us, though.

Actually, he's not such a bad fella, I started thinking. *And he is most definitely good-looking. Possibly I've forgiven him for the other day.*

Hmmm, I wonder what he'd be like to kiss – I've never kissed an African fella before. I'm sorry to sound so coarse but I'm afraid it's what went through my mind.

'Richard,' I said out loud. 'I'm exhausted, I'm going back to the tent. It's just that I'm a bit nervous with all the animals around. Could you come back with me just to make sure I get there safely?' It was a pathetic excuse – there were guards everywhere – but he went along with the story and came with me. Still, there was no way he was going to touch me after being elbowed in the stomach the time before, so on the way to the tent I turned and kissed him, full on the mouth. It was wonderful and after his initial surprise he kissed me right back. Oh my gosh! He was the greatest kisser ever. It was like a homecoming.

But I was still a good Catholic girl. Despite all the B&Ss and one or two serious boyfriends, kissing was as far as I would go. I went to my tent that night to snuggle up alone, thinking about what a great holiday it was turning out to be.

The next day we drove into the Ngorongoro Crater, which must be one of the most magical places on earth. Measuring about 20 kilometres across, it's a massive old volcano that is incredibly rich in wildlife and feels like a lost world, a sort of land that time forgot. For the drive down, I sat in the back with the Irish boys and Claire sat in the front with Richard. None of them knew anything was going on between Richard and me, and so Richard and I signalled each other all day through the rear-vision mirror without their noticing anything. It was all a bit teenaged but it was very cute.

April is not the best time to go on safari in the crater and sure enough we were flooded out, so we headed for the Serengeti where we spent three wonderful days and nights. 'Serengeti' means 'endless plains' and that's what you see when you come out of the crater and over its rim: hundreds of kilometres of swirling grey-brown plains stretching in front of you. At first you don't realise exactly what you're looking at, but then your eyes start to focus and you realise that it's all wildebeest: up close to you and further and further away until the entire landscape is a blurred sea of animals. It's magnificent in its vastness.

A safari in the Serengeti would have to be the world's most romantic setting for a holiday fling. At night, we'd sit around the campfire and the stars were like nothing I'd ever seen before. In the distance – and sometimes up close – you could hear the night noises of the animals: warthogs, giraffes, lions looking for a mate.

Richard could identify everything and always had a bit of trivia about the animals. 'Do you know why the male ostrich is black and the female grey?' he'd say. 'It's for camouflage. The male sits on the eggs at night and the female does during the day.'

I don't know how we kept our relationship a secret from the others. We were both grinning like idiots when the other one was around and there was a bit of tent-hopping – in the most innocent of ways, of *course*.

At the end of the safari we headed back to Arusha and real life came pressing back in. I'd had the fling of my life with the most gorgeous man but I couldn't see any possibility of a future. It would have been easy to let myself fall head over heels in love. What a great kisser! How could anyone resist it? We'd been in the Serengeti, dining under the stars and sleeping under canvas, looking out at elephants while listening to the distant roar of lions. Could anything be more ludicrously romantic? But I've also got a strongly practical side that kicked in and said, 'You work in Uganda, he lives in Tanzania. In any case you did not come to Africa to fall in love and you'll go home to Australia in a couple of years. There is no future here.'

I wasn't even that sure how deeply he felt. Sure, he talked

about undying love and me being the love of his life, but Africans tend to go a bit overboard about love, depending on how well they know their English. They might say, 'I love you, I love you, I love you', when actually they mean, 'You're a bit of all right'. After only one week together, I couldn't take it seriously.

But we had one final night together in Arusha. Claire was tired and went straight to bed so Richard and I and the Irish boys headed out to the Saba Saba nightclub. At some stage during the evening the boys went home but Richard wanted me to see the little house he shared with his brother. We hopped into the zebra Land Rover again and headed out the back of Kijenge to where they lived. It was raining and the lagoon had flooded so we had to park the truck and, with my skirt hiked above my knees, I waded through the water to Richard's two-room house. Richard's little brother, Raymond, was already there, asleep in the one bed they shared. I crashed alone on the couch.

The next morning, we dropped Raymond at school and Richard took me back to Micheli's where Claire was waiting, furious with worry about me. The Irish boys took it in their stride and gave Richard a wink and a pat on the back but Claire was just angry, although I don't think it had occurred to her that anything had happened between Richard and me. It was all a bit of a comedown and we packed our bags for the Arusha Express with a feeling that something special had come to an end.

Richard was at the bus to farewell us and asked me for my address. I thought quickly. I'd had a wonderful holiday romance but I didn't want to spoil it by trying to make it into something it was never going to be. I didn't want to tarnish the memory of what we'd shared. Richard already knew I was working near Masaka but that was a big district. I gave him a false postbox number, safe in the knowledge that that would be the end of it.

It was only on the way back to Uganda that I told Claire about my fling with Richard. She was not very happy with me. It was fair enough – she probably assumed we'd indulged in risky behaviour and we were all very aware of the dark cloud of AIDS spreading over Africa. When we got back, my friend Gertrude, on the other hand, was thrilled to bits about my romance with the gorgeous Tanzanian and didn't let me miss out on any detail of the whole affair, from first kiss to last goodbye.

'You'll see him again,' she said. 'You have to. You're obviously crazy about each other.'

I laughed and shook my head.

CHAPTER FOUR

Term started again, and I turned back to my work with the vigour you feel after a good holiday. If sometimes I was uncharacteristically dreamy or the girls noticed me smiling at nothing, no one mentioned anything. The memory of Richard had settled warmly in my heart but I still felt sure I'd done the right thing by not prolonging the relationship. And I had other things to concentrate on. I'd been coaching the girls in netball and decided to take them to a big inter-school competition, a couple of days' drive to the west, on the Zaire border. Partly, I wanted them to compete in a bigger arena but more, I wanted them to see a wider world. Ugandans are very tribalistic: each area has its own culture to such an extent that it practically has its own language. At the school, when we were organising rosters for the girls' various chores – cooking, cleaning, farming – we were very wary about mixing children from different tribes. I wanted the girls to broaden their view, so this was to be a sort of cultural tour through about six districts with as many languages.

I put the girls – about ten of them – in the school truck and drove them across the country to a town called Bushenyi, near the border of Zaire, for the competition. We slept on the floor in the classrooms of the host school at night and played netball during the day.

Meanwhile, back in Arusha, Richard had written to me a couple of times with no response. The difference between men and women is that any woman in that situation would think, *He doesn't want to see me again – I can't believe I wrote to him*, then crawl away and hide. In the same situation a man thinks, *Well, I know she wants to see me again – there must be some mix-up with the post*. It wouldn't have occurred to Richard that I'd give a false address, so he decided to track me down in person.

If you're travelling in East Africa, between Kenya, Tanzania and Uganda, you can buy an East African passport for a few dollars. Richard had never left Tanzania so he'd never even needed one of these, but now he organised a passport quickly through a cousin at the border and set off on an epic journey. First he caught the terrible, day-long Arusha 'Express' to Nairobi. Then he transferred to the bus from Nairobi to Kampala, which took another sixteen hours. Then at Kampala, he found the big bus station and asked for a bus to Masaka, with no clearer idea than that of how to find me. On the four-hour trip to Masaka, Richard quizzed the bus driver: 'Do you know any Westerners working in the schools round here? Where have you dropped them?'

The bus driver dropped Richard off at Claire's village. Her school had a big volunteer English program and there were often Westerners staying in the village. Eventually, people directed Richard to Claire's house and he knocked on her door. She was so surprised she almost fell over. When she found her voice again, she said, 'What, *what* are you *doing* here, Richard?'

'I really, *really* want to see Gemma,' he said. 'I have to see her. Please show me how to find her, Claire.'

'She's not here. She's away and I don't know where.' Claire was still wary about Richard and cross with me for having kept her in the dark. Then she relented, 'But you could ask her friend, Gertrude. She'll know where you can find her. I'll tell you how to get to the village where Gertrude lives.'

Richard finally arrived at our village, Kalungu, and had a rapturous response from Gertrude, who treated him like a long-lost brother. She washed his feet and clothes, fed him up and, the next day, put him on the first of a series of local buses he would need to take to reach Bushenyi, where I was supervising the girls and their netball.

A couple of days later, I was sitting on the side of the netball court with the girls, watching two of the other schools competing, when I became aware that the girls were giggling.

'Miss Gemma, there's a man over there staring at you,' said one. I took no notice. When you're a Westerner in rural Uganda, you get used to people staring.

'Miss Gemma, he's still staring at you and he's getting closer.' Giggle, giggle, giggle.

I looked up in annoyance. Hang on, this fellow did look quite familiar, and he really was getting closer, walking towards me with his hands out.

When he was about two metres away, he stopped. 'Hello, Gemma,' Richard said quietly.

I was completely stunned, as if I'd been socked in the stomach. It was the last thing I'd expected. '*Richard!* What are you *doing* here?'

'This,' he said. And in front of all the girls, he swept me into a crushing bear hug and kiss.

Boy, did the girls love it! They thought Richard was just the business and were delighted to play their part in the romance. He stayed with us for the final three days of the netball tournament and then came back on the bus with us, in the back with all of the girls. They didn't breathe a word to the Sisters ever, and they always asked me how was Mr Richard going.

As a postscript to that whole episode – about a year and a half later, I saw Richard's fly-catching buddies, Andy and Mike. Andy filled me in on what really happened before that first safari.

'Richard made me promise never to tell you,' he said, 'but I thought you should know now that you're together. When your bus first came into town and you were sitting in the window, Richard pointed at you and said to us: 'Do you see that girl in the window? I'm going to marry her one day.'

Richard had done a little shifty work with Andy and had paid him $50 to make sure he took our safari instead of Andy. I hadn't understood, but it was why they'd always made inside jokes with Richard about $50.

After Richard had found me again, everything changed. From being uncertain about the relationship, I was now sure our future was together – it just felt that is was meant to be. I would have married him on the spot if I could. Apart from being the best kisser and a really genuine hugger, he's someone you just know you can go to if you need anything done. He's very strong and calm. For a village boy from Moshono to travel across three countries to find me was proof of that. He's someone you could drop down into an unknown place and he'll make friends. Even in Uganda, where he knew no one, everyone was his mate.

We had a few communication difficulties in those early days. I didn't have any Swahili – they spoke Luganda where I was – and Richard's English was a bit ropy but we got by. He'd say these gorgeous things like, 'I like your eye moustaches', while stroking my eyebrows, and I'd just have to give him a hug. 'Gemma, learn me more English,' he'd say.

On my side, I'd say ridiculous things when I was learning Swahili. There are two similar words, one meaning angel and one meaning prostitute. More than once, Richard had to lead me off, apologising for me, as he whispered, 'Gemma, you just told that woman she was a prostitute.'

Or another time – and this has to rate as one of the most embarrassing experiences of my life – I was waiting in a bar with some friends of Richard's. I'd been practising my Swahili and wanted to impress him so I asked Richard's friend, a Rasta called Kenyatta: 'How would you say, "You look really sexy in that shirt?"'

'Oh, say: "*Wewe nimzuri sana kitandani*,"' he replied. 'He'll really like that.'

So a few minutes later, Richard walked into the bar. 'Hey, Rich,' I called out. '*Wewe nimzuri sana kitandani*.' Richard spluttered and the room cracked up.

'Who taught you that?' said Richard. When Richard's friends had stopped laughing enough to speak, they told me that my innocent phrase actually meant: 'You're so good in bed.'

Anyway, we managed to communicate. There's never a problem if you're both willing to meet halfway. Now, years later, Richard's English is great, but my Kiswahili, as we call Swahili in Tanzania, still needs a lot of work.

After the netball tournament, Rich went back to Tanzania and his life as a safari driver and I went back to Kalungu village and mine as a school teacher. But in both of our minds, we were together. I was never concerned by our time apart or worried that he might find someone else because I knew Richard had such a strongly ethical character. He's not a churchgoer but he's very upstanding. Some of the other safari guys in town would have had to go into triple digits to count the number of Western women they'd been with, but Richard was too wholesome.

Whenever he had a break between safaris, Richard used to try to come and visit me. He was extremely well-mannered and respectful, so he never came near the convent. Instead, he'd stay with one of the teachers up in their quarters and I'd go and visit him. But I'd always be back in my single convent bed by ten o'clock. I think some of the Sisters suspected something was up, but as long as neither of us abused their trust, they turned a bit of a blind eye.

It was very expensive for Richard to be constantly border-hopping, and in those days he was only earning a few dollars a day as a driver. So I made sure that every school holiday I'd go down to visit him in Tanzania. Often, Richard would be in the middle of a tour group and we'd arrange to meet at whatever campsite they were visiting. I'd take the local bus out from Arusha to where Richard was and walk until I found the camp. It never bothered me to travel alone on some of the worst buses in Africa to find his campsite and have only a few hours with him before he had to drive on with his clients to the next national park.

It was a good way for me to meet local people and improve my Swahili. One of the places we often stayed was Twiga's campsite near Lake Manyara. While Richard took the tourists to the national park for the day, I'd stay behind with Mr Twiga and talk to him or his cook, trying to pick up as much as I could.

I knew things were beginning to get serious when Richard took me out to meet his family. Richard is the oldest of seven children and comes from a very solid, family-oriented background, not unlike mine if you discount the thousands of kilometres and cultural differences separating Moshono from Guyra. As the eldest of his family, Richard had been expected to marry early – to a suitable local girl – and start having children. Richard's father is the chairman of the village, and so Richard owed it not just to his family but the community to ensure that the Sisia name would continue.

But he hadn't. By the time Richard and I met, he was in his late twenties and there wasn't a lasting relationship in sight. His family was beginning to be very worried and he'd been given a serious lecture by his father, his uncle and another respected man in the village. Baba – as Richard calls his father – sat Richard down and said: 'You need to find a wife. You're getting too old to be single. We will help you find a suitable woman.'

Baba is from a Maasai background, and in his day the parents often chose a bride for their sons.

But Richard knew what he wanted and was respectful yet very clear to his father. 'I am from a new generation,' he said. 'I do not want my wife to be chosen for me. I don't even think I want a Tanzanian wife at all from what I've seen of them. I want a woman who is educated, one who is looking towards the future, not just a clothes-horse who is going to sit at home and wait for me to bring the money in.'

'And where will you find this woman?' Baba asked, a little disbelievingly.

'I don't know,' said Richard. 'But when I do, I will bring her home to meet you and then you will know that she's the one I want to marry.'

Of course, I was completely unaware of this conversation or the fact that such a weight of expectation was placed upon my visit. Richard bringing a girl home! That had never happened before. And a Western girl at that! That was something worth bringing the whole family together for.

They couldn't have been kinder. It was Christmas and even though the family didn't have much money, Mama – or Bibi as we call her – had made a beautiful lunch on a big table outside the hut, with goat stew and rice and salads. The whole family was there and they'd laid lunch out under the trees. Everyone was dressed in their best church clothes and they treated me as if I was a queen.

And I was as sick as a dog. On my way there, I'd felt the first chills that heralded the onset of a bout of malaria, but I hadn't wanted to turn back and disappoint anyone. By the time we sat down to lunch, all I could do was lie around in the dirt, sweating and shivering. I managed to eat a tiny amount, then fell asleep on Richard's shoulder while he was talking to his family. Malaria really saps your energy and, even though some distant part of my brain said I should be trying harder to impress my potential in-laws, my body had just shut down.

Despite the poor impression I must have made, the fact of having appeared was enough to satisfy his parents. It was the first of many happy visits to Moshono over the next few years.

One of the reasons I love Africa is that it appeals to the risk-taking side of me. Life here is precious because it is lived so fully – and precariously, not cautiously and prudently as we do in the West. To realise this, you only have to drive a car on any African road: no one obeys any road rules or speed limits or even stays on the right side. Their cars are completely unroadworthy and yet as drivers they're probably more skilled and with quicker reflexes than someone who has been schooled in a more sedate driving environment. You're always aware here of being poised on the knife-edge of existence and it makes you grateful for small blessings and aware of the part fate plays in your life.

One holiday, Gertrude and I decided that we felt like spicing up our routine teaching lives with an adventure. We thought we'd avoid the killer buses and make our way to Tanzania on a ferry across Lake Victoria, which would then join us up with a bus at Mwanza. From there we'd travel around the national parks. We pre-booked the ferry, the MV *Bukoba*, and then, on our way to catch it, Gertrude decided that, as she'd never left Uganda before, she'd better ring her father to tell him exactly where she was and what she was doing.

Now Gertrude's father lived in a little village where there was no telephone. Nor did we have one. So we had to head back into town to the post office where Gertrude put in a call to the post office in Mbarara, a larger town near her father's village. They in turn had to send out a boy to cycle the five kilometres to Gertrude's father's village, to bring him back to ring Gertrude in Masaka. I was used to these sorts of complicated, time-consuming arrangements by now but, in this case, it was excruciating because there was only one ferry a day and time was ticking.

We waited and waited. I was becoming more and more frustrated. We only had a few hours before the ferry was due to leave and I knew we were going to miss it as we were still a few hours away from the wharf! At last, Gertrude's father rang back and they had an infuriatingly inane conversation: 'Isn't it exciting? I'm going to Tanzania across Lake Victoria!' And so on and so on. Gertrude hung up and I dragged her onto a local bus heading to the ferry wharf, but it was too late. We had missed the boat and would have to wait for another day. I was furious with Gertrude and we settled down to sleep on the wharf in frosty silence.

As we waited for another ferry, some news came filtering through and the wharf started to fill with wailing women. The *Bukoba*, which we'd been booked on, had sunk, only a few kilometres short of Mwanza. It had been licensed to carry 300 passengers but that trip it had strained under 1000. More than 800 people had drowned.

Our escape is one of many things that gives me faith in a higher power. If Gertrude had just happened not to telephone her father or it hadn't been such a difficult business, we would have been in time for our ferry and probably been killed. As it was, it gave the nuns who knew of our travel intentions such a fright that they forbade me to make any more trips outside Uganda for the rest of my stay.

It didn't stop me seeing Richard though. We had some lovely teachers from northern Uganda at the school and they'd invite me to stay with them during the holidays. Then they'd cover for me as I nicked out of the country and down to Tanzania, to Richard.

Gertrude and I still managed to have a lot of fun, often just escaping the Sisters' radar. I took their car one day to drive into Kampala on official school business, buying supplies. Gertrude came with me and, while we were in town, we thought we might as well make a night of it and go dancing at a nightclub. I pulled the car up right outside the club, totally forgetting that the Sisters of the Sacred Heart logo was proudly emblazoned across its side. The next day, one of the Sisters took me aside.

'Gemma,' she said. 'I've heard a little whisper that our car was seen outside a nightclub in Kampala last night. As I can't think how that can have happened, I won't say any more about it, shall I?'

'No, Sister,' I said. In truth, I was already calming down from my old B&S days. I probably only went out with the teachers once every couple of weeks and even then I was back home by about 10.30 pm. I was growing up, I suppose.

At the end of my time in Uganda, just before Easter 1997, my brother Benn came out to stay with me and to travel around together as part of his last hurrah before he got married. It was a wonderful time for me. Benn and I had always been inseparable and I loved introducing him to my life in Africa. And, of course, to Richard, which had made me a little nervous. Benn was the first member of my family to meet the man I loved and I wanted so much for them to get on well. Especially as Richard's family had welcomed me with such open arms.

At first things went brilliantly. Benn, Richard and I went down to Zanzibar, a magical island off the coast of Tanzania, and the three of us had a great time, fooling around and swimming with the dolphins. They're both such boys, quite similar in some ways. They even shared a similar sense of humour. One night at dinner, Richard asked Benn whether he needed a fork.

'*What?*'

'Would you like a *fork*?'

'Not with you matey I wouldn't,' said Benn. Both of them thought they were hilarious with that one.

Then I dropped a small bombshell. Benn and I were alone, talking about this and that, when I said casually, 'Oh, and Benn? I'm pretty sure that Richard's the one. I want to marry him.'

He didn't take it seriously at first. Richard was a great bloke, and Benn was pleased that I was having such a good time in Africa, but that was where the relationship and Richard were going to stay. Richard had no idea about our culture, about the way we lived. I was going to come home, I'd meet a nice Aussie boy and that would be that.

When I made him realise that I was serious, Benn was very thoughtful.

'Gem, you've been stuck in this Africa rut for a few years now. I know you really love it here and part of that is thinking that you love Richard. But can I ask you to do one thing first?'

'What?' I said.

'Come back to Australia with me. Take yourself out of this situation and have a break. If you're still thinking about Richard after six months or a year then, okay, there's something there. But it's too serious a decision not to give it real consideration.'

I didn't like Benn's advice but, knowing how much he cared about me, I gave it proper thought. I hadn't looked at another man since meeting Richard and couldn't see that changing. But I'd finished my time at the school and drained my credit card dry. I had to return home to Australia in any case.

I still intended to come back to Africa as soon as possible but I wasn't exactly sure how I was going to manage it or in what capacity. I knew I wanted to be with Richard forever, but Benn's response had made me realise I'd been a little naïve to imagine that he would be welcomed with open arms by my family.

At some level, I also knew that my work in Africa had just begun and that, as satisfying as it had been teaching the girls in Uganda, at some stage I wanted to make more of a difference to the people who needed it the most.

When I left him, Richard said, 'I'll see you in Australia, Gemma.'

'Yeah, right, Rich, whatever. Just don't worry about it. I'll be over by Christmas to see you.'

'You don't think I can do it?' he asked. 'Remember how I came to find you in Uganda? Don't think I can't find you in Australia. I'll do it. One day you'll look out your window and a big black man's going to be walking up your driveway.'

I desperately wanted to believe him but it seemed unlikely. I flew out, feeling like I'd left the most important part of me behind.

CHAPTER FIVE

When you're moving through your own life, sometimes you don't see patterns emerging until you've gained enough distance to look back on them. From up close, everything is chaotic, but step back and your random choices form something approaching order and direction. Situations that at the time may have appeared pointless reveal themselves as the useful steps along the path that they were.

It was like that with my time back in Australia after I returned from Uganda. What could have been a wasted period – in the great scheme of my future life in Africa, with Richard – actually proved to be the key to everything I would later do.

As soon as I got back, I found a job in Armidale, the largest town near my parents' property, at NEGS (New England Girls' School). I got a foot in the door through tutoring, and then a science and maths position came up and I was given it.

I loved the work and the girls and consequently had good results with my students, even though it was a very different environment from the village back in Uganda. The girls I taught were in years 10, 11 and 12 – they were 15–17-year-olds, so I found I had more success if I treated them as equals rather than as students. As Dad used to say, I always liked finding shortcuts, and as a teacher I was no different from the student I'd been, organising the study groups at university. These girls were bright and sensible so I found it saved a lot of time to give them their own syllabus to work from. It made them much more accountable for their own learning and they took charge of what they needed to know, never letting me miss a thing.

'Miss Rice, we haven't covered point two,' they'd say. Or, 'It says here we need to do a diagram as well.'

I'd say to them: 'I want you to go to the back of your exercise book where we have the recipes for how to answer different types of maths questions. Today we're going to do simple equations. Here is the question, these are the steps to solve it and here are five examples.' The girls would have to do the examples, then turn back to the front of their exercise books and do a few sets of exercises before we'd move on to another type of equation.

I would never go into the theory behind the equation unless it was in the syllabus and the girls appreciated this. I remembered that at university I'd often thought it was pointless going to the lectures, as most of the time the lecturers would just make the concepts more confusing. It was better for me to get the syllabus, research it myself and then find every existing past exam paper in the world to practise. Keeping it simple for the girls meant getting through the syllabus easily so that we'd have plenty of time to go through hundreds of past papers. Everyone flew through their exams. The school was happy, the parents were happy, and the girls felt confident about maths and science, which often isn't the case.

Obviously there are many other, probably better, ways of teaching. The head of maths at NEGS, Shirley Cook, who became a great friend and mentor of mine, was a genius and my complete opposite. She understood the theory behind everything and would often explain it to me without ever sounding condescending. She was a great head of department and, even though we were different, allowed me to teach my ways. The kids knew where they stood, and it worked.

Soon after I arrived back home, I spoke to Father Ferdie, who'd helped me find a job in Uganda in the first place. I wanted to tell him about my time at the school because his niece had also worked there and he'd always been a mentor to me.

'Well, Gemma,' he said, when I'd finished talking, 'now that you're home, what are you going to do to continue helping these people?'

It was something that had been concerning me. 'I just don't know, Father. What can I do? I'm just by myself, it's not like I'm an organised charity.'

Father Ferdie was a little old man, only about five foot in his habit and sandals, but his drive far overshadowed his small stature. 'You can always do something,' he said. 'Even if it's to help just one person.' It was how he lived, believing nothing to be impossible, right up until his death.

That reminded me of Winnie. 'Actually, Father, there is something I wanted to do. My great friend Gertrude has a very intelligent little sister. I would really like to raise the money to complete her schooling and also to send her to university as she wants to do law and I think she could do it.'

'Right,' said Father Ferdie. 'That sounds worth doing and it sounds like something you could easily organise. Now let's see you do it.'

Now I had a plan, I was fine. The next weekend I visited Dad down in Kyogle (where he'd been working in a law firm since the wool crash) and opened a bank account with a grand total of $10, my first contribution towards Winnie's $2000-a-year school and boarding fees. I knew there was no way I could pay her fees on my own – after almost three years away, I couldn't even pay my MasterCard bill – but I was sure I could rope in some support from family and friends. I ordered 20 deposit books from the bank, the idea being that everyone who wanted to help would get a deposit book so it would be easy for them to pay in a regular sum – five dollars a month – and I'd have a record of who deposited the money.

Armed with my new deposit books, I went home for the weekend. Mum, Father Ferdie, Bishop Kennedy and Mum's friends Patsy and Rhonda each took one. I wrote to Winnie to let her know that we would help her with her education and get her to university as well if she got the right pass.

There was a lovely Filipino priest in Inverell called Father Joe. He'd come from a pretty rough background in the Philippines and was doing as much as he could to help children in the next generation. I asked him if I could come and give a talk to his parish about the money we were trying to raise for Winnie, to see if any of them would like to hop on the bandwagon. He agreed and a few more people took books.

Then fate stepped in and lent a hand to our fledgling charity. Looking back, I would now call it a St Jude moment. The head of the English department from NEGS, Maree King, and her husband, Don – who, incidentally, were my brother Benn's future parents-in-law – were out to dinner in Armidale one night. Another lady at the restaurant, a Mrs Clark who was there with her husband, Neville, suddenly felt unwell and had to go outside. Maree went to her aid and the two husbands followed them out. Mrs Clark recovered and the two couples ended by dining together. It transpired that Neville Clark was the Rotary Governor for the Rotary District 9650. After Maree told him a bit about what I was trying to do, he contacted me to ask whether I'd be interested in addressing his district's annual Rotary conference, a very big ball game, with an audience of 500 or more, representing some 30 or 40 clubs. When you speak at a district conference, those representatives then report back to their clubs, so it's a great way to reach a large, ever-expanding number of people.

I hadn't realised it before but Rotary is an amazing organisation. I had no idea of the scale they operate on internationally and the amount of aid they provide. They've raised about $600 million to eradicate polio worldwide, and they have almost succeeded, with only a few hundred spot fires left to put out. Once that project is completed the next thing on their agenda is eradicating malaria. I'd only really associated Rotary with having sausage sizzles at the country shows and sponsoring picnic sites, which is great but not in the same league as ridding the world of diseases.

I was a bit nervous about addressing such a big gathering but it was an opportunity that I couldn't turn down. And I'm glad I went. Thanks to my years of public speaking and then teaching, talking to an audience felt completely natural to me. I went on to talk at the Inverell, Tamworth and Armidale Rotary clubs. All Rotary clubs in towns all over the world have weekly meetings and there has to be a speaker at each meeting. In a small town, they can get pretty hard up for notable speakers. Having come back from Africa, I was suddenly hot property around the local Rotary clubs who were desperate to find a speaker for their weekly meeting. It was a wonderful win-win situation – they needed me but not half as much as I needed them for Winnie's education fund.

Wherever I spoke, the good people who make up the Rotary clubs immediately got behind me and took deposit books. From there, things started to snowball. I started speaking at Rotary and Inner Wheel clubs all around our district and suddenly, from my initial $10, I now had about $200 a month pledged, with more coming in all the time. I had to contact the Sisters in Uganda so they could find a second and a third girl to receive a free education, thanks to all the people who were coming on board to help pay for their school fees. They were delighted to help, and more girls joined Winnie at the Kalungu Girls' Training Centre.

Our local bishop at the time, Bishop Manning of Armidale – who'd succeeded Bishop Kennedy on his retirement – also offered me his support. He helped me place articles in our local newspaper and invited me to talk to the people at Armidale cathedral. Bishop Manning was later transferred to the Parramatta Diocese but he continued to support us by personally sponsoring a child and organising for his new diocese to do the same.

While studying, Winnie sent thank you letters, which I photocopied and handed around to all involved. In time, with our continued financial support, Winnie, who had been head girl of her school, went on to study law and opened her own office in Kampala, so you could say our investment in helping kick-start her future really paid off.

Meanwhile, I missed Richard terribly. A few people, including Father Ferdie, tried to set me up with nice young men in utes to give my thoughts a different direction, but without any success. There was no one else for me. I don't think there ever could be. However, it was also a very happy time. I was living in Armidale in a big old house with half of my brothers – all the bachelors – and Dad would stay a few nights a week instead of driving back out to the farm. At around this time, Dad moved from Kyogle and opened a law office in Armidale, which for a man in his sixties was quite a big call. But he never gave up, which was so typical of my father. He and Mum were such great role models for all of us children.

So it was all men living in the house – except for me – and I loved it. It was like the old days. In addition, I'd have my brothers' friends all dropping in, hoping for a dinner. I had a Malaysian cookbook and sometimes I'd experiment on the boys with that. There was one particular friend of my brother Paddy's who'd stick his head in while I was cooking dinner and ask: 'Is tonight a cookbook night, Gem?' If it was, he'd stay. Otherwise, on chops, mash and peas nights, he'd say, 'See you later,' and head back out. The boys went out quite a bit so I often had to put their meals aside for them and have my dear Dad to myself, just the two of us, making it a special time in my life I'll always treasure.

All this time, Richard still said he was going to come out to see me at Christmas. *Yeah*, *sure*, I thought. Every now and then he'd call with an update. He had a passport. A few months later, he had an Australian visa.

'That's nice, Rich,' I'd say.

But suddenly, he called to let me know that he had a ticket and a flight number and was actually arriving in Sydney. He really *did* have a passport and he had somehow scraped together the money – I later discovered that he'd mortgaged his Land Rover to a friend's safari company – and decided to fly across the world, which was very gutsy of him.

When the day came for Richard's arrival, I drove down to Sydney, thinking, the poor bloke's hardly been out of Arusha, let alone East Africa. It will be a miracle if he reaches Sydney without getting lost. I imagined him arriving at the airport and his confusion if he couldn't find me and was determined to be there in plenty of time to pick him up. So once I left Armidale I took a shortcut over the mountains to avoid the delays on the New England Highway.

This was one shortcut I should not have taken. As I rounded a bend, I saw cars banked up ahead and workmen holding 'Stop' signs. They were building a new road and were blasting rocks out of the mountainside so it was too dangerous to pass. For an hour and a half I waited, at first patiently, then anxiously and, finally, beside myself with frustration. To pass the time, I started talking to the boy who was holding the 'Stop' sign and, by co-incidence, discovered that he'd just returned from a trip to East Africa.

'*East Africa!*' I cried. 'I'm on my way to Sydney to pick up my boyfriend who's coming here from Tanzania. He's never left East Africa before and if I don't get to the airport in time to meet him, he's going to be totally lost!'

Fortunately the lollypop boy was sympathetic to my story. Between blasts, he somehow managed to sneak me past the workmen's barriers. I put my foot down like you wouldn't believe and flew to Sydney.

I arrived at Sydney Airport, abandoned the car in the car park and ran into Arrivals just as Richard was emerging from Customs. It was so good to see him, like rain after a drought, or coming home after being away longer than you meant to be. I just ran and threw myself on him.

Poor Richard had been feeling very nervous. Back in Arusha, Richard is a big man about town. Wherever you go, you hear people calling him, 'Bob Rich, Bob Rich', a reference to his well-known love of Bob Marley. But travelling to Australia, he was a lone African man, at the mercy of every petty customs and immigration official who seem to delight in giving Africans a hard time. Leaving his familiar environment, he'd become a very small fish in a very large pond, and when he arrived his customary confidence had briefly deserted him. But once he'd seen me, he knew everything was going to be all right.

A couple of nights later, Richard had totally recovered, and was entertaining the crowds at my brother Dan's pub in Balmain.

'Where are you from, mate?'

'Africa.'

'Far out – where in Africa?'

'Tanzania.'

'Wow, Tanzania – what do you do there?'

'I'm a safari-driver.'

And the questions poured in thick and fast: 'Do you see lions every day?' 'What about elephants?' 'Have you ever been attacked?' 'Are you allowed to shoot them?' 'How high's Mount Kilimanjaro?' 'How big's the Serengeti?'

I had to do a bit of two-way translating – Richard's English wasn't yet up to a barrage of Aussie accents in a noisy pub – but he was in his element, surrounded by blokes, nursing a cold beer, talking about the life he loves. In fact, during Richard's entire stay in Sydney, no one was anything but positive and friendly. Of course, he wasn't applying for a job or residency so we weren't really testing people's tolerance – that might have changed things.

It was so exciting to show Richard around Sydney. Seeing everything through his fascinated eyes gave me a new appreciation of simple things, like the range of products in a supermarket. When we visited the Opera House, there was a plane writing an advertising slogan in the sky with smoke and Richard took probably half a dozen photos of it. It was all so new to him.

And then we went home to Wyoming for Christmas. Wyoming Christmases are very dear to all of us. We have them every second year and everyone – sons, daughters-in-law, grandchildren – makes a big effort to get there. It's chaos but wonderful chaos. There's about seven bedrooms in the house, then one family usually goes in the big horse caravan and another brings a campervan. We always keep 15 or 20 mattresses on the verandah for drop-ins, so all the kids grab their sleeping bags and sleep all over the living room floor.

In all the usual pre-Christmas mayhem, it was hard to see how my family were receiving Richard. He seemed to be getting on well with my brothers and Dad and the sisters-in-law were all gorgeous and welcoming. Mum was harder to read but so much of the work and preparation fell to her that we didn't have much time together to talk properly. But it was important to me that everyone liked Richard because I suspected – not that we'd formally discussed it, but I knew – he was there for a purpose: to ask my father if he could marry me.

It's hard to imagine a more awkward situation in which to ask for someone's daughter's hand in marriage. Whenever Richard thought he had Dad to himself, a rogue grandchild would pop up, or Mum would need Dad for something. It's difficult enough getting up the nerve for that interview with the prospective father-in-law anyway, but in a thirty-odd-strong household, it was nearly impossible to get him on his own. At last, Richard saw Dad striding off towards the machinery shed, alone.

'Right, I'm doing it now,' said Richard, determination written all over his face.

'Okay, good luck,' I said and watched him disappear after Dad. A quarter of an hour went by, then half an hour. Finally, after three quarters of an hour, the two men emerged looking . . . not exactly happy, not exactly downcast, more a little bit unsettled.

Richard told me the gist of the conversation later. When Dad had realised what Richard was asking, he said: 'Well, Gemma's very headstrong and the fact that you've been able to stay together for this long does you credit. Do you know that she wants to marry you?' And Richard said that, yes, he did.

'Gemma's done some crazy things, but she's never really made a bad decision in her life, so if this is what she wants then I know

Mum and Dad at their wedding in 1959, on Australia Day. Mum's parents are on the left, and Dad's are on the right.

Mum made the matching tops we wore on this visit to the beach when I was three years old.

My big brother Benn and I were inseparable as children.

My family visited hundreds of agricultural shows when I was growing up. Here Dad is holding my hand, with Matthew on his shoulders. On the horses (from left) are Tim (on Magician), James (on Magnafeet) and Nick (on Dion).

From the time I could walk until I went away to boarding school, horses were my life. Here I've just won Girl Rider in the 15- to 17-years age group at one of the local agricultural shows.

Crutching sheep with my brothers Paddy, Benn and Danny.

A family friend sitting in the garden at Wyoming, amid the rock work that Mum made with her own hands.

A sheep sale on the family property.

Our home was an open house, and friends and visitors would often sleep on the verandah.

Benn and me, the morning after one of the many B&S balls we attended together.

Ballerina and me in the Mud to the Dust endurance race, which covered 560 kilometres.

With Ballerina and her baby, Basil, who had been born only minutes before, in the middle of the race.

At my graduation from the University of Melbourne with Mum and her mother, Nan, on whose 60th birthday I was born.

This calf cage that I built for the ute while I was at university was one of the few things I'd constructed myself before embarking on building a whole school!

Bishop Kennedy and Father Ferdie, two of the most wonderful male mentors in my life, besides my father.

With my wonderful team of brothers at Nick's 40th birthday. Back row (from left): Nick, Dan, Matt and Benn. Front row (from left): Tim, Paddy, me and James.

My sewing class in Uganda display the first items they made.

Ready to set off on my first safari. Richard is standing, with Iddi, the cook, behind the boxes. Claire, the Canadian fellow and I sit on the hood.

My friend Kathy poses with the little motorbike we rode to see the gorillas in the Impenetrable Forest in southwestern Uganda.

This was the last time I saw my dear friend Gertrude. She died six months later.

Dad and Richard in the woolshed at home, during Richard's trip to Australia in 1998.

Christmas Day at Wyoming, 1998. We had a ball trying to fit everyone in our large family onto a wooden pallet.

The piece of land my father-in-law gave me, on which the school would be built.

Day Two of construction of the first school building. A Rotary volunteer team helps dig the foundations.

On my wedding day with my brother Paddy, who gave me away.

Following the ceremony, the wedding party gathered outside the Catholic church in Moshono village.

Rather than a traditional wedding cake, we were presented with a cooked goat, fully skinned save for its hairy head.

Richard's Maasai relatives, singing during our wedding reception.

My nieces and nephews gather around while I sew sheets, curtains and baby needs on the peddle sewing machine a few months before giving birth to Nathaniel.

Richard and me with Nathaniel, after bringing him home from the hospital.

Nathaniel, fascinated with the beading the Maasai women wear.

Where do we start? Richard and me, sorting through boxes of donated goods, 2001.

Another early struggle was building an entrance road for the school, so all our vehicles weren't bogged like this one! Now more than a dozen school buses travel this road every day.

As well as building a school, we still needed to eat!

Angela with our first three students, Said, Leon and Sia, on the first day of school, 2002.

she has her reasons and that those reasons are sound. I respect both of you. But I can't really give my approval without talking to Sue and I'm afraid that she's not going to like it.'

So it wasn't to be the open-armed approval that we'd hoped for. Dad was in a very difficult position because he wasn't against Richard and my marrying but he couldn't encourage it while my mother was opposed. And, as feared, she was aggressively opposed. I vividly recall her actual words: 'I will never, *ever* give my blessing to this marriage.'

Equally against it, strangely enough, was my darling brother Benn, who'd always been my playmate and ally in all adventures. Mum, I could sort of understand. With only one daughter, she was loath to lose her to the other side of the world. She comes from a very conservative, religious background and lives in a small country community. For her only daughter to marry a black African and go to live in the back of beyond seemed inconceivable. There I was, private school- and university-educated, announcing my intention to live in a two-room hut made of bamboo in a place nobody had heard of. Probably with chickens. I suspect that Mum was worried about 'what the neighbours will think' along with her justifiable concerns about my happiness and wellbeing.

I tried to discuss her concerns with her but kept running into a brick wall. What infuriated me was that she kept saying how surprised she was that I suddenly wanted to marry this man, when I'd hardly ever talked about him and didn't even speak to him on the phone that often.

'But Mum,' I said. 'Every time I mentioned his name you sighed or rolled your eyeballs.' I had just wanted to keep the peace so of course I'd rarely discussed him with her. It was easier to keep quiet and speak to Richard only when no one was around.

Benn, on the other hand, just thought we were making a terrible mistake. He liked Richard as a person but wanted no part of him as a brother-in-law. He was about to get married himself to a lovely local girl – no opposition there – and I think he still thought I was as much in love with Africa as with Richard himself. With hindsight, I can see that Benn was frightened he would lose me, not just geographically, but that I would change into someone unrecognisable.

It was a very difficult time. We were trying to get ready for Benn and Bianca's wedding, which was something we were all happy about, but underlying it were the beginnings of the worst rift I'd known in our close family. Mum said she didn't want Richard to come to Benn's wedding and Benn, for whatever reason, didn't stand up to her. Rather than be the cause of continuing friction, Richard made a polite exit and returned to Tanzania. He had been supposed to stay for seven weeks but had been in Australia for barely a month.

I drove Richard down to Sydney, both of us flat with disappointment and sadness, but returned to Wyoming for Benn's wedding, alone. I was still sure Richard and I would one day marry but I didn't want to marry him in the face of my family's opposition. I know it sounds old-fashioned, like something out of a nineteenth-century novel, but I wanted both my parents' and all my brothers' approval. I loved and respected them and, even though I knew Mum was wrong about Richard, I still valued her opinion. So I stayed in Armidale, working at NEGS, bringing in donations for Uganda and waiting. Waiting for my mother to change her mind.

CHAPTER SIX

With Richard gone and our hopes of marrying in the near future dashed, I was glad I had something positive to concentrate on: the Ugandan education fund. If I couldn't be in Africa, at least I was doing something constructive for some African children.

I was speaking at a lot of Rotary clubs and district conferences, and news of our charity was spreading. All of a sudden we had hundreds of people taking deposit books – we had given out more than 900. We had money coming in left, right and centre and could put dozens more children into school. I would often leave work at NEGS in the afternoon and drive non-stop to speak at a town a few hours away, then stay at a Rotarian's house only to wake up at 4 am and drive back to Armidale for another day's teaching. I have never turned down a speaking event unless I physically could not get there. You never know what might come out of speaking to a person, if not immediately, then at some time in the future. I will talk to an audience of 1000 one day and just as happily to five people the next day

– it all spreads the word about the educational needs of children in Africa.

My father saw the explosion of donations and warned me that this was not just a little family effort anymore and I could get in trouble if the group did not become recognised by the government. So he helped me make our group effort into a registered Australian charity. As well as fixing tractors and crutching sheep and arguing his case at the bar, it just so happened that Dad was great at writing constitutions and organising boards of directors. So our little band of fundraisers became officially: the 'East Africa Fund', charity number CFN 16123. On top of that, wonderful Kevin Pike from the accounting firm Roberts and Morrow in Armidale said that they would do the yearly auditing of our accounts for free. To this day, even with the school so large, Roberts and Morrow still do the auditing of the accounts free of charge (however, I don't think Kevin ever imagined it would become so big so fast when he first made that offer).

It was a very exciting time but I also realised how quickly you could lose control of an organisation like this. The Sisters in Uganda were wonderful but by now we were also dealing with other schools, primary and secondary, and even helping some students on to university. We were helping between 100 and 150 young people, some by paying their full tuition at school, others with one-off payments to tide things over when times were tough. The charity was sending on close to $50,000 a year. I would send the money directly to the institutions but it often never arrived – or rather I suspected it had arrived and the head-mistress had dined out on it rather than paying fees. The children would write to me, telling me that the school wouldn't let them attend, and when I contacted the school they'd say that the child's fees weren't paid. People were also sending their children to schools which I had not approved and so all the arrangements were getting out of control. It was sad that the Sisters' efforts had to suffer because of people around them taking advantage of our desire to help. It was also incredibly frustrating being stuck back in Armidale and not being able to see exactly what was going wrong. I decided I would have to fly over to Africa.

I had no money but I couldn't let a little thing like that stand in my way. Also, I had to see Richard, after the debacle of Christmas and the proposal. I formulated a scheme to lead a tour group to Africa. If I organised the trip for seven people and each of them paid a little more than the actual cost, then the fare for my trip would be covered. I took people who were already supporting children there through the deposit books and who wanted to see an Africa that a normal tour wouldn't offer them. My friend Gertrude agreed to be my tour guide for Uganda and Richard, of course, would take care of the Tanzanian end. We'd fly into Egypt, then on to Nairobi, Kenya, where Richard would pick us all up and take the group into Tanzania to go on safari in the Ngorongoro Crater and the Serengeti plains. He'd then help me take the group to the island of Zanzibar, to swim with dolphins in the turquoise waters. From there we'd fly back to Entebbe, Uganda, where the Sisters had agreed to lend me the school truck I had driven many times when I worked there. Accommodation would be free because we'd stay with families of the kids we were helping. The way we arranged it, none of it was expensive, but it was a gorgeous itinerary and enabled me to check on what was happening to the money we'd been sending to people in Uganda.

The plan worked perfectly. With Richard as our guide, we had a fabulous time in Zanzibar and on safari. It felt completely natural and normal to be with Richard again and our tour group loved him.

As we travelled I was thinking all the while about the charity and trying to find a solution to our problem with the missing money. One idea – and it seemed like a pipe dream – was to cut out the middle people and build our own school. I still assumed that I would build it in Uganda. I already knew the area and there were lots of people there who really needed help.

Then Richard and I drove out to see his family. We stayed at Richard's new little bamboo hut which he'd built himself on a plot of land his father had given him. He had built the bare frame of sticks but there was no mud on the walls so we had to pitch tents inside. We called it the 'mosquito house' – for reasons that were only too obvious.

On that trip, Richard's father said something extraordinary to me. *Baba*, or 'Father', as I now called him, is a patriarch, a very strong man and the village chairman, but he also believed, unusually for someone from a Maasai background, in the importance of education.

The Maasai are traditionally hard, shrewd people, whose main concern is expanding their herds of cattle and having many children to many wives. But Baba was different. In marrying Richard's mother, who was from Kilimanjaro, he'd already allied himself with someone from a different background, and he had encouraged all his children to gain as much education as they could. By this stage, I was very close to Richard's family. I know that they might have wished we'd hurry up and get married but I always felt completely welcomed by them.

Baba and I went for a little walk around the village, through a field of ripening corn.

'Richard has told me that you're helping a lot of children in Uganda,' said Baba as we strolled. 'Now, that's wonderful, and we're proud of you. But what about the children here? Tanzania has many poorer children than Uganda and you are almost my daughter-in-law. Why can't you help the children here in Moshono?'

I'd never really thought about it but he had a point. In Uganda, because of a government policy that allows free primary schooling for four children per family, at least 80 percent enrol in primary school, while 12 percent make it to high school. Not very impressive statistics, but better than Tanzania's with only 60 percent enrolling at primary level and just 5 percent continuing to secondary school. Around Arusha and the local village, Moshono, there were some government schools but they were hopelessly overcrowded and underfunded.

Richard had been to one himself and had told me about classes of 100 or more students, with teachers who – because they often weren't paid – frequently failed to turn up and, when they did, were underqualified and often violent to the students. Richard had somehow made it through primary school and into secondary school, but he had to get up at 3.30 every morning to walk through Arusha and up into the mountain to the closest secondary school. Some nights, he was too tired to make the return journey and would camp out by the river with his friends. Unsurprisingly, he never finished high school. And this was an education system that was expected to equip students for life in the 21st century in Arusha, an increasingly sophisticated city of more than half a million people, where computer skills and English are a minimum requirement for employment.

In the face of such a hopeless situation, without money or contacts, what could I do? 'But Baba,' I explained, 'Uganda's where I started. It's where my contacts are.'

Baba stopped walking. 'What if I gave you a piece of land?' he asked. 'Do you think you could raise enough money to build a school for the children in this village?' We were standing waist-deep in corn. 'This field measures half an acre. Could you build a school on this half acre?'

'Um . . . Yeah, sure,' I said, without thinking.

'Then it is yours,' said Baba.

I looked at the field and up at the craggy peak of Mount Meru. Fields of bananas bordered the corn and the ground under our feet looked rich and fertile. For a moment I could see it: the solid brick classrooms, the grassy playground, children on swings, voices chanting times tables floating on the air. *Sure*, I thought. *I can build a school here. Just a little school, for the village kids.*

I even had a name for the school ready to go. For me as a young, white Australian woman to build a school in a cornfield in Tanzania and make it successful, I'd need all the help I could get – especially from my old friend, the patron saint of hopeless causes.

'Thank you, Baba. If you mean it, I'll try to do it. We can build a school here and it's going to be called The School of St Jude.'

How hard could it be?

That trip to Tanzania proved life-changing, as did our subsequent visit to Uganda. The moment I arrived, I knew something was wrong. Gertrude was supposed to meet us at the airport but she never turned up, which was out of character. I drove to visit her family in their village, five hours away, the surprised tour group in tow, and they told me she was in hospital, but didn't tell me why.

As soon as I saw her in her hospital bed, nothing but bone and skin, I knew what was wrong: AIDS. There was so much of it in Uganda. It's one of my strongest memories from my first trip there. There were funerals every two or three weeks, always for the young people. The only good thing was that at least Ugandans were usually open about the disease. In Tanzania, it's never mentioned. There's always a polite fiction that so and so died of 'tuberculosis' or 'cancer'; the disease is never named for what it is.

When Gertrude and I first met, she had just started going

out with a nice boy, Joshua, who worked at a nearby school, St Henry's. About a year before I came home, they announced their engagement and were about to throw a big party. Just before the party, Gertrude found out that Joshua had had a drunken one-night stand with another teacher from St Henry's. He was beside himself with guilt and so apologetic, but Gertrude was a strong-minded girl with a lot of self-respect. 'If you've done it once, you'll do it again,' she said, and didn't take him back.

Six months after the party, the other woman had died of AIDS.

When we heard about her death, Gertrude was horrified. 'God, what if I have it?' she said.

'Well, you might have and there's only one way to find out,' I had replied. 'Just do the test.'

But she wouldn't. She was too frightened of what she might discover. So now here she was, so thin and fragile, clearly dying, but still my same old mate Gertrude inside. We took her out of hospital and the group helped me cart her around with us in the truck. Frail as she was, she loved being with everyone. And God knows, I loved seeing her. We still shared a mattress, just like when I'd slept over at her place in the old days. But she was so sick. One of the people on the tour had two children who were doctors and once we were home they started sending over medicine for her, but by then it was too late to save her.

Before I left Uganda with the tour group, Gertrude said to me: 'Gemma, don't forget your dream about starting your own school. You can do it. And when you do, don't forget to teach AIDS education as well.' It was probably the last thing she said to me.

I returned to Armidale with Gertrude's voice still in my ears and immediately initiated a new fundraising campaign, to start building the school. Also, the tour had been such a success that I immediately began to plan a second one, not least to make sure

I'd see Richard again within the year. I organised a 'Buy a Brick' campaign, where people could donate money towards building a school in Moshono. All the Armidale, Tamworth and Inverell Rotary and Inner Wheel clubs had stalls in their town, and school students knocked on every door in Armidale. By the end of that weekend, we'd raised about $20,000.

People think building a school sounds romantic. I suppose there is a romantic element, the story of something being created out of nothing and then the potential that school has for completely changing lives, but really, building a school is mostly just hard slog. The last five years since the school has started have taken more out of me than all the years before put together.

Then Armidale Central Rotary Club came forward and said they would help organise a team of volunteers to go over to start building classrooms. Moshono is only a small village, smaller even than Guyra, and I thought that two blocks of three classrooms would certainly be sufficient for a little village school. My older brother Nick, who is a building contractor, supplied an architect, who designed the first block for free. We based its sawtooth roof design on the roof of a woolshed at Longreach in Queensland where my father once owned a sheep station. It gets pretty hot out there and Dad figured that a roof that kept an Aussie shearing shed cool, light and well-ventilated would work just as well for an African school, without the need for expensive electricity.

A great friend of my family, David Steller, who was an engineer with Armidale Council, offered to lead the team and there was a young builder, Tyson Jackson, who'd just finished his apprenticeship, but apart from these two, the main building qualification of the first team that went over was goodwill. There were a few teachers who knew me, some university students, even a couple of school students. I'd gone to Barbecues Galore and picked up a pile of tents and a couple of portable showers and so, carrying their own accommodation with them, the team set off for Tanzania. I couldn't afford to go with them as I was still having fun paying off my credit card from my stint in Uganda, but the team assured me they would document everything with pictures and phone calls.

Richard picked them up from the airport. Then he drove David Steller around Arusha buying wood and spades and wheelbarrows and all the other bits and pieces necessary for starting work. He also organised ten or so fellows from the village to come and help the visiting team.

I really, *really* wanted to be with them but there was no way I could stump up that plane fare again and I had to be realistic about it. I gave the team my camera and asked them to take as many pictures as possible of every single thing, and they did. Every step of the work was documented, from the first day's corn harvest to ready the field, through digging the foundations and laying the first bricks. Every day they'd hold up a poster for me: Day One; Day Two; Day Three. It was miraculous what that team did in such a short time. Richard had a mobile phone by this stage so I could ring every day and check progress.

By the end of two weeks, we had one classroom block divided into three classrooms, with brick walls, cement floors and timber roof trusses. No roof, though – we'd run out of money – but hey, you can't have everything. We later sent the money over for the iron sheets for the roof and the Tanzanian builders we'd worked with put them on.

We then raised money for a second Rotary building team to go over and build the second classroom block. This time the team was about six or seven couples from the Gosford North Rotary Club. Before they left Australia they met David Steller and were given instructions about how to build the block, with a few modifications to finesse the design. When they arrived, the men set to work setting the new foundations, while the women painted the doors and window frames built by the first team. By the end of that team's visit, we had a second three-classroom block: floors, walls and roofs but no plaster, no electricity, no paint on the walls. You think that by the time you get the bricks up you're almost there, but you're actually just beginning.

All this time, Richard had been continuing to live his life in Moshono. He had bought his own safari truck years before, though he was still paying off the mortgage he'd taken on it for his ticket to Australia, and was working for himself – a much more lucrative line of work than driving for others. He was also finishing building the little bamboo hut where I'd stayed when I was out with the tour group. It was completely my decision that we had to wait for my parents to come round to accepting our relationship, but Richard was very patient. But by this stage, he was in his mid-thirties and there were beginning to be rumblings in the village that things could not go on like this.

Richard is the eldest of seven children in his family and that's a responsible position. His younger sister already had a child, and another brother had two. If, in Australia, a man is still single in his thirties, his parents might be a little concerned. In Africa, where people marry much earlier and are very family-oriented, it was a cause for real alarm. There's no such thing as a pension or superannuation: your children are all you have to support you in your old age.

Richard's father and the other big men in the village summoned him to a meeting. Richard had no idea what it was about but soon found out, as his father sat him down.

'We've decided that the time has long since passed for you to get married. You must choose a wife and do it now.'

'But Baba, you know that Gemma and . . .'

'Forget Gemma,' Baba said. 'That's never going to happen. Be realistic. Why would she leave a first-world country and come and live in a third-world country with you? Why isn't she here now? The time has come for you to face your responsibilities and forget about this stupid dream. You will marry a Tanzanian woman and act as the son of a village chairman should act.'

Baba had always seemed very fond of me, but after so many years he must have thought I was never going to settle down. I'd just been out to Tanzania leading another tour group but I'd left again. It was too unsettling. Richard owed it to his family and the village of which he might one day be chairman to have a wife and children.

Richard was calm and firm. 'I'm going to marry Gemma, whatever you say. Please don't try to make me marry someone else. I will not do it.'

What could they do? Richard was a physically and mentally strong adult and he'd stood up to his elders in a very untraditional way. They did the only thing they could and backed off gracefully.

I suppose Richard's stance strengthened my resolve. I'd kept him waiting too long. *I'd* been waiting too long. Two years after Richard had asked my father for my hand, I put my foot down with my parents and said, 'That's it. I'm sorry you're not happier about it but Richard and I are getting married with or without your blessing.'

It wasn't as though Richard and I had had a fleeting romance. By this stage we'd been together for more than six years. We knew each other well, we'd tested the relationship through separation, and it was stronger than ever. But still Benn and my mother tried to make me doubt what I was doing. They operated as a team. Clearly, they'd discussed the issue at length and worked out the questions they wanted to ask me, because when either one was alone with me, they'd bring up the same things: 'What about your work? What will happen when you get older? What about when you have children?'

I was hurt by the idea of them colluding but I still had a faint hope that some of the family might be brought around by the idea of a wedding, now that it was a reality. The response was underwhelming. Benn was certainly against my moving to Africa and wouldn't consider coming to the wedding. The older boys, Tim and James and Nick, were noncommittal. While they wished me the best of luck, they had young children and no intention of coming out to Africa at any time in the near future. I understood and truly didn't mind a bit. The twins planned to come out. They're both very adventurous and great travellers. As it happened, Paddy made it to the wedding and gave me away, but Dan was injured in a brawl at a pub he was managing so he didn't make it.

Dear Mum's response was just plain odd.

'I've spoken to the priest here, Gemma,' she said, 'and he's told me that the land where you're planning to build the school is evil. Two bad men are buried there and they didn't make their peace with God before they died. I don't know whether it will be enough to save it, but as my wedding present to you and Richard, I'm giving you nine masses to be said for the school.'

'Mum,' I said. 'I know you've never wanted me to marry Richard, but this is ridiculous. There aren't any graves at the school, I've never heard of anything so crazy. However, if you really want to give us masses for our wedding present, that's great. We need all the support we can get.'

I hadn't expected her to be enthusiastic, but I certainly hadn't expected to hear that the school was cursed. But after that conversation, I didn't give it another moment's thought.

Just before I left, Dad took me aside and quietly slipped me a cheque for $1000. 'Here, Gem. Put this towards your wedding,' he said. I don't know whether or not he told Mum. I would have loved him to have given me away.

Leaving for Africa this time was strange, almost an anticlimax. This was something I'd been waiting for, dreaming about for such a long time, but now that I was finally on my way to live in Tanzania with Richard, I didn't feel much of anything. A bit of relief, if anything, a feeling of 'finally we got here', but some of the excitement about the wedding had been blunted by the long wait. It's not that I wasn't excited about marrying Richard or starting the school, it's just that organising the wedding itself seemed more like one last hurdle to be overcome.

I needn't have been concerned. Weddings in Tanzania are as unlike Australian weddings as it is possible to be. I'd never been to an African wedding so my first experience of one was as a bride, and that's a strangely relaxing position to be in. In that area of Africa the bride does nothing for her own wedding. I mean *nothing*. There's a wedding committee, formed of all the groom's closest male friends and relatives, and they do everything. First, one of them organises the wedding contributions so that all the guests donate money to pay for the party. Then one boy organises the decorations, another does the food, a third orders the drinks, a fourth writes the invitations. My whole role in this was to answer the occasional question: 'My favourite colour is blue', or 'I like goat', or 'Yes, I do think we should have a mix of music.' As we were simultaneously trying to finish the building work on the classroom blocks, this level of involvement suited me perfectly.

So my wedding day was like a wonderful piece of theatre, where I didn't know what was going to happen next: it was fascinating and exciting and exhilarating at the same time. All I was told was that the wedding was at 3pm and that someone would pick up my bridesmaids and me at midday to take us to the hairdresser. I had Leasa, my boarding-school friend out from Cootamundra, Claire, the English girl who'd been initially disapproving of my relationship with Richard while on safari, Kathy, with whom I'd motorbiked to see the gorillas, and another Lisa, a local girl who works for a safari company here. We had a hilarious time together, especially at the hairdresser, who had a great range of groovy patterned head shaves and synthetic hair extensions on offer but absolutely no idea how to deal with Western hair. We ended up doing each other's and doing not a bad job. After changing into our wedding clothes at Lisa's, we were picked up by a car completely covered in blue ribbons and balloons and white roses. Because of all the rose farms here, roses cost next to nothing but the car looked a million dollars.

So we piled into the car and were taken to Moshono church, where we were married by the Kijenge parish priest, Father Chuvi. Tanzanian etiquette says that if you receive an official invitation to a wedding you have to bring a present, but other than the invitees, anyone can turn up and expect a plate of food and some local brew. The Moshono church is tiny and on that day, with a local boy marrying a Western woman, it could not have fitted one more curious onlooker in. It was chockers, hot and steamy, but it was so much fun. The Kijenge choir, half of whom grew up with Richard, sang, unaccompanied, in perfect pitch and rhythm and it was beautiful.

Then came the next local ritual: a crazy, noisy procession of cars up towards Arusha and back, with thirty or so safari trucks, all with their tops off and people playing trumpets and honking horns. Supposedly, the bridal couple isn't meant to show much emotion on their wedding day but I know that, sitting in our car, watching our friends and family hanging out of the open tops of the safari trucks, riding over potholes and seeing all the kids waving and running alongside the procession, I was grinning like a lunatic.

We did a U-turn before we hit town and headed back to the village. The classroom blocks were still bare and unfinished but we had the reception on what would one day be the school's verandah. The boys from the wedding committee had made a big stage and covered it in blue and white fabric. Everywhere there was the heady scent of wild lilies, which some of Richard's friends had collected on the mountain. It was beautiful.

By the time we got there, there were crowds beyond crowds. We'd budgeted for about 400 people but there must have been almost 1500. We ran out of food, we ran out of drink. It was a great day. My mother-in-law, Elizabeth, is from Mount Kilimanjaro, where the women traditionally brew a sort of banana beer. About 60 women had been busily making vats of that for days. It ran out too.

Every moment was a surprise. There was an MC in charge and he'd announce what would happen next: 'Okay, now it's time for presents!' And everyone would line up to come up to the stage to bring us a present. Baba's side of the family are all Maasai so they all came up doing the incredible Maasai jumping, leading goats with one hand. We were given goats and chicken, fabric and vegetables. It was such an experience.

Then came the best part. Everyone started chanting, 'CAY KEY CAY KEY CAY KEY' and I wasn't sure what was going on. I worked out that the wedding cake must be coming and looked around for something white and iced, maybe with a little model of the bridal couple on top. Well, the Tanzanian notion of a wedding cake is a little different. As the calls of 'CAY KEY' reached a climax, I saw a goat being wheeled out. It had been cooked and fully skinned, except for its head, which was still hairy. The goat had been propped on its haunches and squatted there, looking blindly at me. That was my wedding cake. Richard and I had to feed bits of it to each other in turns, symbolising, I suppose, caring for each other in married life.

The tradition is that after the husband and wife feed each other, they feed the bride's parents but, in their absence, Richard cut off some nice meat and fed it to my brother Paddy. Being his usual playful self, Paddy, in response, pretended to cut off the goat's balls and feed them to Richard.

We had so many guests from overseas that we'd decided to forget about trying to have a honeymoon on our own, so we headed off to Zanzibar with about 20 friends for a week. But then it was time for them to go back to Australia and England, and time for us to return to Moshono, my new home. I had six months to get the school ready for its first students – we were due to open at the beginning of 2002.

Until now, seeing Richard again and marrying him had occupied most of my thoughts; I hadn't had all that much time to think about the school. When I had contemplated it, I was overwhelmed by how much I had still to do.

It was time to stop planning and start doing, right here, right now. For so long I'd talked about the life I hoped to have in Africa. Now, I was living it. Richard and I were married, we had a life together, we were a family. The school was on its way to becoming a reality. My life's work in Tanzania had begun.

CHAPTER SEVEN

'And when did you plan to enrol your child, Mrs Sisia?' the registrar of Green Acres Academy asked.

'Oh, we don't have any real plans at the moment. We're just doing a bit of research, looking to see what's out there,' I said.

I was a bit evasive about the details, but it was true that we were doing research. Pretending to be interested in enrolling our son, Richard and I had made appointments with a few of the local schools, checking out their facilities, how their classrooms were set up, what the fees were. It wasn't for our own child – though in fact I was already pregnant – but for my other baby, the school we were building.

The schools we were looking at were the best of the African-run private schools. We weren't aiming to compete at the level of the expat schools, where the children of UN officials went, but at the level of the schools for the middle classes of Arusha, the children of the doctors and lawyers and safari company operators. I was not especially impressed by what I saw.

Compared with even the most poorly funded government school in Australia, these schools were dismal. There was no space for children to play. Rooms were bare and stark, without artwork on the walls or anything that suggested learning might be fun. Everything felt utilitarian and neglected, down to the ugly, uncomfortable-looking chairs in the classrooms.

I didn't see why that had to be the case, even when the children you were educating were from the most humble of backgrounds. I knew that you could get away with the bare minimum in terms of comfort or aesthetics – after all, these were not children with high expectations or experience of life as anything but a hard struggle – but if you put in the bare minimum, then that's probably what you'd get out. I've always liked to do things to the full, following my parents' maxim that nothing's worth doing by halves.

So if you're going to create a place for the children to play, then it should have decent equipment, painted bright, cheerful colours, that invites them to explore. The playground should be a good size, with trees for shade and to soften the institutionalised look of bare brick classrooms. Classrooms should be light and airy, uniforms neat and smart. All of these things foster children's sense of ownership of and pride in their school. They give the school its culture, its identity.

For example, one of our biggest initial expenses was a school bus. We knew we would need one before we opened the school, so darling Richard sold his Land Rover. This was a very big sacrifice. When you own your own safari truck, you make US$120 a day from taking people on safari. As a driver of someone else's truck, you make US$5. But, as Richard said, 'You can't have a school without a school bus,' and he traded in his truck for a little white bus. Of course, it had done about a million kilometres and was falling apart, as has been every subsequent bus we've bought here. But Richard is very handy with mechanical things, and by the time he'd put on new tyres, new springs and new shock absorbers, bought some scrap metal and had it welded to the body of the bus, it was good as new. Well, it still looked like rubbish, but it went all right.

Not long after school had started Richard asked, 'What colour would you like the bus painted?'

I thought for a minute, and said: 'Royal blue, because it's going to be the school colour.'

And on the side and front of the bus we had the school's name written in swirling gold: The School of St Jude. It was another small detail that cost next to nothing but created one of our most recognisable school symbols: brightly coloured, easily identifiable buses.

Little touches like that helped not just the students but also the staff to feel pride in our school. Painting the buses bright colours cost no more than a drab white or grey, and it made everyone feel good. There has never been any extra money in the kitty at St Jude's and in those early days we were always sailing right at the edge of disaster, but we tried to make things look good on half the money.

We still had quite a job to do. Those first Rotary volunteer teams had built the shells of the first classroom block but they were just shells: brick walls and roofs. We needed plaster and paint, electricity and plumbing. And then there was the small issue of selecting the children to start at the school in January 2002. Oh, and finding some teachers, ideally well-qualified, disciplined and caring, who were pleased to work for a pittance.

I had never built anything in my life – unless you counted a guinea pig cage when I was ten and a calf cage for the ute when I was at university – let alone built something in a third-world country, with unqualified builders, using a language I could barely speak. I was very lucky with the first builders Richard found for me – it must have been beginner's luck because we've probably been through 300 since. One of the men looked about 85 going on 400 years old and the other about 16. I know now that their names are Charles and Very, but at the time we called them the old builder and the baby builder. '*Fundi*' is an all-purpose Swahili word for tradesperson – you have a car *fundi*, a sewing *fundi*, a wood *fundi*, a brick *fundi* and so on. Charles became the cement *fundi*, with the task of plastering the brick-work. '*Toto*' is Swahili for 'child'. So Very became '*toto fundi*' and it stuck. He's now built every truss, window frame and door in the whole school and has been an essential part of our building team for five years.

With the classroom blocks on the way to completion, I started to think about the sort of children we wanted to educate at St Jude's and where we were going to find them. Fortunately, by this stage I had the support of some amazing volunteers.

One of the biggest and most thankless tasks in this period was sorting out a huge container-load of *stuff*, most useful, some useless, that had arrived from Australia, shipped out by the Rocklea and Armidale Central Rotary clubs, who are still helping with containers to the school to this day. While I was still in Armidale, teaching at NEGS, I had let people know that I would welcome the donation of any goods that might be useful for a school. Every day I'd come home to find boxes of books, fabric, stationery and miscellaneous bits and pieces left on my doorstep. I'd then lug it down to a storage shed on Saturdays, and when I had enough boxes I borrowed a horse truck belonging to one of my brother's friends. Some of my school students from NEGS would come down on Saturdays and help go through all the donated goods to make sure that what was going to Africa was worth taking there. Then Rotarians from Armidale Central

Rotary Club helped me load the boxes into the horse truck and I would drive it to Brisbane. It was laden with hundreds of boxes, mostly filled with books, and they were so heavy I nearly burned the brakes out on a big mountain range between Glen Innes and Tenterfield.

I'd given the books an initial sort-through and discarded such useful texts as *The Economics of the French in the Nepalese Highlands*, but when the container arrived there were still piles and piles of boxes, inside which were piles and piles of books, lacking any order whatsoever. This is where I think St Jude stepped in and sent me an eighteen-year-old boy called John Southwell from Narrabri, who said he'd like to come over to Arusha for six months to help the school in whatever way he could.

John was the opposite of me, methodical and pedantic. He was the perfect person to go through the container and put all the pens in that pile, pencils in this pile. He sorted out the primary books from the secondary, the textbooks from the readers, and then tested every pen and texta to make sure it was in working order. The downside to being a charity is that you have to accept every donation that comes your way. Often someone would donate their child's old pencil case but you'd later find it was full only of dried-out textas, pencil shavings and an ancient apple core. Sorting out containers is finicky and exhaustingly boring, and John was a godsend.

And so the weeks slipped by, in a mess of books and desks and plaster, with two competing deadlines looming – the start of the new school year and, before that, the birth of our first child.

I hadn't had much time to dwell on my pregnancy, but that is more the African way. Women here get no special concessions for being pregnant and work right up until birth. The one thing that

Richard made me do during pregnancy was eat an egg and drink a glass of milk a day which, being unrefrigerated, unhomogenised and unpasteurised, was fairly disgusting. I did it for him but *errrgh*. In the West, women are much more pampered during pregnancy but are left to fend for themselves after the birth. In Africa, you mightn't get special treatment while pregnant, but you receive wonderful support from the whole extended family after you've had the baby.

I did have a lovely obstetrician, Dr Kamaro, who is known locally as the 'baby doctor'. He had gained his degree in Dar es Salaam, Tanzania's commercial capital and largest city, and then studied obstetrics in the United States but, unlike a lot of doctors who qualified overseas, he had come back to help the women here. It was free to go to him for antenatal checkups, then it cost a mere $50 for the delivery at the Arusha ICC Hospital. The Arusha ICC isn't a Western-style hospital – most Westerners would go to Nairobi to have their children – but it's an average hospital for wealthier Tanzanians and the largely middle-class Indian community. If you couldn't afford to go there, every village had a medical clinic staffed by a doctor and a nurse.

I sailed through my pregnancy with no complications, able to give my undivided concentration to getting the school ready to open. Then one night in early October 2001, Richard and I were at home in the 'mosquito house'. I was cooking dinner when suddenly I felt something, a different sort of cramp from the twinges I'd felt throughout the pregnancy.

'Rich,' I said. 'I think we're going to have a baby.'

Richard gulped. 'Really?' he said, looking nervous. 'I'll go and get the car out.'

I laughed at him. 'Not right this second, silly. But I think I just had a contraction.' Then I stopped laughing as another one started. They began as a tingle, then the tingle became a pain, then the pain became a jabbing. By about midnight, I felt that we should get to the hospital. We arrived and dear Dr Kamaro laid me down on a steel trolley – none of your soft sheets and pillows here – and told me that I'd hardly started. 'You'll probably have the baby around lunchtime tomorrow.'

I didn't want to believe him but he was right. Looking back, I was incredibly lucky with my first labour. The hospital was deserted, so instead of being in a ward with ten other labouring women, I was on my own. And because we were the only ones there, the nurses relaxed their usually strict 'no men' rule so Richard was able to stay with me for the whole labour. I don't know how they manage it but African women labour silently, while lying down. There was just no way I could lie down. The pains were too strong and the only relief I found was by walking up and down the room. There were no drugs on offer, so the way I coped with the contractions was to hug Richard from behind and really squeeze his stomach. Poor Richard allowed himself uncomplainingly to be used as a beanbag.

By 11.15 the next morning, the pains were becoming unbearable. 'You've still got a long way to go,' said my nurse. 'Don't worry, you can handle it.'

I was just so tired. I was at that stage when women often want to give up and go home. 'I don't think I'm ever going to have this baby,' I said to Richard.

He took my transitional ranting seriously and started crying. 'Don't die, Gemma. Please don't die. I'm going to fetch the doctor. Just please don't die.'

'I'm just tired,' I said. 'Not dying.' But he'd already gone for the doctor.

When Dr Kamaro returned with Richard, he said the magic words: 'You're about to have the baby.' And Nathaniel was born on 3 October 2001 at about 11.30 am, all 4.6 kilograms of him.

Richard had had a Maasai blanket around his shoulders, just for warmth, and we immediately wrapped it around Nathaniel. Our little treasure was so beautiful.

I felt weird and amazing. I couldn't believe I'd done it. I couldn't believe he was ours. He had beautiful coffee-coloured skin and black hair and big, dark brown eyes. He looked like both of us, and neither of us, and himself. Like all babies, I suppose.

Only one day later, Nathaniel and I went home, just as another girl came into the labour ward, which was excellent timing. At home, Mama, Richard's mother, was wonderful. Without my own mother there to help me, she showed me how to bathe the baby and massage him with coconut oil and how to clean round his umbilical cord.

'But you must not let the cord come off in his nappy, Gemma,' she warned darkly.

'Why is that, Mama?'

'Because if it does and it touches the penis, the baby will grow up *gay*,' she said, completely serious.

'Oh, okay,' I said.

So every day she'd ask: 'Is it off yet?'

And I'd say, 'No, Mama. Maybe tomorrow.'

The umbilical cord finally came off after a bath and on the change table so everything was all right and Mama could look forward to another generation of Sisias.

Once we were home, the procession started: brothers and sisters, aunts, uncles and friends came in, all wanting a look.

There's a great local tradition that men aren't allowed to touch a baby until they've brought him or her a present, so all the men brought baby powder and coconut oil and little blankets and kangas – the brightly coloured lengths of fabric people use here for everything. It was gorgeous. The men, great big thumping safari drivers and farmers, all picked him up and passed him around, cooing and smiling. African men are so comfortable with babies, perhaps because they've come from large families and are used to looking after little brothers and sisters. Richard was immediately at ease handling Nathaniel, where I felt very awkward at first, as if I was doing it all wrong and the baby would break.

Traditionally, the new mother is supposed to stay at home for the three months following the birth of a baby. Everything is arranged to make sure that the mother is well-rested and healthy and can focus on feeding the baby, which makes sense in a country where most people couldn't buy formula or, if they could, would have little chance of sterilising bottles and purifying water. During this time, her husband is supposed to bring home as much meat as possible, to buy it if he can or kill it if he has to. The mother-in-law looks after all the washing of the materials used during the birth, the bathing of the baby and the cooking of the meat into gallons of broth, in the belief that drinking broth helps the new mother produce milk. So I had goat broth for breakfast, lunch and dinner, which thankfully I didn't mind. Tradition also dictates that the sisters-in-law do the washing and cleaning of the house for three months.

A couple of days after giving birth, this tradition sounded pretty good. But the second day after I got home, I had a call from Richard. He had applied for electricity for our house two years previously. After jumping through various bureaucratic hoops, greasing palms and stopping just short of murdering someone, Richard had just been told that the electricity company was finally on their way out to Moshono with five poles and our wires.

'I know you've just had a baby, Gem, but I can't be there. Could you supervise? Oh, and another thing, the health inspector has called to say that they're coming to inspect the school.' So much for being cosseted and feeding the baby. I trundled out in my dressing gown, holding Nathaniel, to tell the electricity blokes where everything should go. It was actually all fine, and once they'd gone we were able to pirate the electricity and redirect it to the school. We'd been waiting for the electricity to be connected for so long that by the time it was, the excitement had worn off a little. But it did make things a bit easier at home with a baby.

We were still living in the 'mosquito house' which now had proper plastered mud walls and three rooms, including a bedroom which Richard had added on for our wedding. We still had bucket baths – there was no running water – and cooked outside on an open fire. At least now we were able to have a fridge – no more room-temperature milk. It honestly never occurred to me that my early married life was unusual or difficult in any way. It was all an adventure. When volunteers came out to work at the school, it seemed natural that they'd stay with Richard and me, and Nathaniel now that he had arrived.

About six months before I came over to marry Richard, I had gone to my old school, St Vincent's, to speak to the Year 12 girls at their farewell breakfast. I told them a bit about the work I'd done, raising money to send children to school in Uganda, and then about my plans for a school in Tanzania. At the end of my talk, a lovely young girl approached me. She said her name was Angela Bailey and that she'd love to come over to help me open the school. I didn't really take her seriously. She was only 18, a beach girl from Coogee. Lots of young people say 'I'd love to do what you're doing' but you never expect them to follow through.

Ange was different. First, after leaving school, she enrolled in a six-month diploma in childhood studies – the quickest possible qualification she could find. Then she came on the first tour I ran to Africa. I showed her and the group where we were going to build the school and, again, she said: 'I really want to come and help you open this school.'

I'd got to know her quite well on the tour and discovered that she was very vivacious and great fun. I knew that she'd be an asset to the school. Apart from anything else, beggars can't be choosers – I needed all the help I could get. It's not as though I knew what I was doing myself.

'I'd love for you to help,' I said. 'Just get your qualification, and get over here, girl.'

So Ange finished her diploma and contacted me to say: 'I'm still coming; I'll be there for the new year.'

I picked her up on New Year's Eve and took her home where she lived with Richard, Nathaniel and me for most of the next two and a half years. Ange slept in the lounge, Nathaniel slept in our old bedroom and Richard built on a new bedroom for us. It was quite easy to add on another room, because the bamboo sticks are interlockable. It's like building with Lego.

In those early days, we had a lot of young volunteers coming through and they all basically lived around our house or in the storeroom at the school. John Southwell, the one who was sorting the container load, lived for his whole six months in a Barbecues Galore tent in the garden. There were always three or four tents dotted around the house. We had a roster on our fridge and every day someone was in charge of cooking lunch while another person cooked dinner, which was a bigger job than it sounds, involving going to market, lighting a fire and cooking on the open flames. Later on we built a house especially for volunteers to live in, with ten bedrooms and a communal dining and living area, which transformed the lives of people visiting; but those early days with everyone mucking in together were very happy.

Living communally was never a problem for Richard or me. We're both from big families and, in any case, in Africa families rarely operate as a nuclear unit. There are always grandparents and aunties and cousins mixed in. Our house is only a couple of hundred metres away from Richard's parents', which is lovely, especially for the grandchildren. But all the same, particularly when you're living so closely, there have to be boundaries. Richard's mother and father have never been anything but lovely to me and respected our privacy, but there were a couple of occasions early on when I had to draw the line with Richard's siblings. Not so much the older ones but the teenagers, who wanted to show off to their friends that they had a white sister-in-law.

When Nathaniel was about one month old, I walked into my house to discover Richard's little sister Deborah and four of her friends making themselves at home. They had the music going full blast and were looking through all my books and photo albums. I just said 'Welcome', but with a look that made it clear how I was feeling. She never did it again. Another couple of times, I'd come back to the house and be about to start cooking our dinner only to discover the meat I thought was in the fridge had been taken by one of my brothers-in-law, plus a litre of milk to go with it. That sort of thing is quite acceptable here – people use each other's stuff all the time – but I soon managed to get the message across that it wasn't acceptable to me.

However, I really appreciated that not one of Richard's family ever, ever asked me for money. Usually if an African man marries a Westerner, his family will think, *We've won the lottery here.* That has never happened and, in fact, Richard's family has given me so much, from the land for the first classroom blocks onwards.

They've also been very lax in what is expected of a daughter-in-law. For example, there's a local tradition that the daughter-in-law should take a hot pot of food to her mother-in-law every night. Well, I tried it for a while but, with the school and Nathaniel being born and Mama being such a dynamo herself, she told me to stop and said kindly that she didn't really need the help. I'm not sure what that said about my cooking.

Elizabeth is goodness personified and a beautiful mother and grandmother. She not only had her own seven children but raised another six, mostly the result of relationships that didn't work out or one-night stands. People here are quite religious – clearly not religious enough to stop them having sex outside of marriage, but religious enough not to use contraception or to terminate an unwanted pregnancy. And the dominant role of men – who don't take 'no' for an answer and wouldn't dream of using condoms – means that a lot of young girls get pregnant unintentionally. Mama has ended up with some of these children or has fostered them until their mothers were able to look after them properly. Now she's also bringing up her grandson, Hans, whose mother died of AIDS a couple of years ago. So she was a wonderful support to me when I came home with Nathaniel.

I certainly needed the help because I had to concentrate on what was always going to be one of the toughest jobs at the school: selecting students. We had two finished classrooms, with 25 chairs in each, sitting empty. I didn't want to fill them up with children who weren't going to make best use of this opportunity.

It seemed to me that the children who were most likely to get the most out of a good education were the ones who were bright and really poor. I would love to have been able to help educate every child in Africa but that was clearly not practicable. The next best thing was to make sure that each dollar we received was going to go as far as possible to improve the lives of as many people as it could. I've always thought that the poorer people are, the more drive and determination they have. They are also more bound to a place, through necessity by poverty but also through long ties of family and community. Every child deserves a good education, but educated middle-class Africans are more likely to take their qualifications and leave the country, rather than stay and use them where they're needed.

An early decision I had to make was that we could only take one child per family. It wasn't an easy decision, especially when a bright student often had equally clever younger brothers and sisters, but again, I had to be practical. One child with an education could make a big difference to a family, changing the prospects of all its members. He or she could support their parents in their old age and help the younger members of the family, with the benefits spilling over into the whole next generation. I'd rather help two families than one.

I was very new to Tanzania and had no real contacts outside Richard and his family, so I asked myself who would know who was really struggling around the village and needed help. I thought, at home people put on a brave face but it's the parish priest who often knows what's happening behind closed doors and who's suffering. So, a bit naively, when I wanted to start up our child sponsorship scheme I went to the leaders of the three core religions in town. First I went to the parish priest and asked for a list of Catholics around Moshono whom he knew to have fallen on really hard times. Then I went to the mosque and asked the sheik for a similar list of Muslims. Then I visited the Lutherans and asked for their list of children in need. We've never selected our students on religion or tribe: we are influenced only by aptitude, attitude and poverty levels.

So I had a lovely list of 30 hand-chosen children, which was great – until I noticed that the first name on the sheik's list was his son, Muhadini. Then I recognised a few of the other names as children who were associated with members of the church board. I realised that the lists were corrupt and couldn't be relied on. I also realised that if we couldn't trust the religious leaders, we could take no one's word about their circumstances. We would have to check on every individual child who came into the school.

I started going to the mosques on Fridays and to the churches on Sundays and approaching people directly, saying: 'If you have a child in your family who you feel is gifted but you can't afford to send to a good school, then bring them round to the School of St Jude next Wednesday and we'll give them a bit of a test. If they qualify and if you're hard up enough, we'll give them a full scholarship to the school.'

So we began to get queues of kids and their parents coming to the school on Wednesdays, ranging in age from 2 to 25 years. At first I thought that ideally I'd like to take children from as young as four, to give them the best foundations, but I soon realised there was no foolproof way of testing the aptitude of children as young as that. We decided to focus on seven- to eight-year-olds, old enough to have learned a bit in their government schools and to be able to complete a simple maths and reading test.

It felt like Ange and I were in the office every day until night, testing children. There were an awful lot of them but not many who fitted our quite specific criteria. Some children might be bright but you could tell from the way they were dressed that they were from a well-off background. Others would be clearly poor, with dull eyes and bad skin that gave away their inadequate nutrition, but unable to work out which way on the test was up. Or they might be bright enough and poor enough but were ruled out by being too old.

As the start of the school year approached and we were finally ready to open, we had a grand total of three children: Said, Sia and Leon. However, on the first day of term Said turned up late.

Ange and I were beside ourselves with excitement as the bus rolled in – and two tiny children climbed down.

'Hello,' said Ange, and one little one promptly burst into tears. We were so consumed with the mechanics of the day that we forgot to take many pictures, and because they were only little the children went home at 12.30. Ange and I were exhausted. We both collapsed into bed at 6.30 pm, saying, 'How are we ever going to run a proper school when it's so tiring with just three children?'

It didn't stay that small for long. As soon as word spread about the school and that we were providing a free Western-style education for poor children, I had parents camping out on the grass outside my kitchen wanting me to let their children in. The queues for testing, which we'd moved to Friday, were phenomenal. Sometimes they were even frightening, when the crowds of children were big but parents kept pushing more and more children into the crush. We soon discovered that people would do anything to get their child accepted into the school.

I also discovered that some people are poor because they just don't care for themselves or their children. Ninety-nine percent of Tanzanians are very proud, in a way that we can't imagine. If you go to their house, even though the floor is just pressed earth, it has been swept and their few possessions are spotlessly clean. Then there is the 1 percent who are poor because they can't be bothered. We had a few children from families like that that we took on, then they'd turn up in dirty uniforms or without their exercise books or not at all. It might seem harsh to give someone the possibility of a future only to take it away again, but why should another deserving child miss out on an education in favour of a child and their family that don't appreciate the chance they've been given? And so we continued to refine the selection process until we had roughly the procedure we have today.

First the children would come in on a Friday to do a reading test, in Swahili, and then a maths and simple spelling test. You get hardened to the process, but weeding out the children at this stage is emotionally challenging. African children have a very different sense of personal space from Westerners. They would nestle right into you as they read, often laying a trusting little hand in yours. You can never forget how important this is to each child, what it means for their future. The ones stumbling over their simple Swahili are no less adorable than the ones flying through, but if we allowed ourselves to be swayed by that we wouldn't be able to do our jobs properly. It was very hard, though, especially at the beginning.

If they passed the tests, the children had to go home and return with some documentation: exercise books and reports from their government school and some sort of proof of age and identity. Most children in rural Tanzania don't have birth certificates and often they'd bring a baptism certificate in its place. Even these we had to scrutinise carefully. It's very easy to bribe an official, even a religious, to falsify documents in Africa. So we checked and double-checked and triple-checked: was the name on the exercise book the same as the name on the certificate? Were the exams and the exercise books from the same school and in the same handwriting? Do the numbers four and seven that the child wrote on their entrance test look the same as those in their exercise books or did an older sibling do their test for them?

Once we were confident that the child was who they said they were and that they were the age their documents claimed, we'd visit their family at home, first to confirm we had the right child, then to make sure that the family was both poor enough and had the right attitude.

On the whole, children don't lie unless someone is putting them up to it, so we did our house checks in pairs: one of us would talk to the child and the neighbours outside the house, and the other to the parent inside. If the two sets of information didn't correspond, then we'd know something was suspicious. People were so desperate to get into the school that they'd try anything. To qualify for sponsorship at St Jude's, children had to come from very poor backgrounds. If their house had a cement floor, running water, windows or more than two rooms, they didn't get in. So sometimes, a child would take you to 'their' house – a one-room mud hut – but none of their possessions would be there. The mother would be unable to produce any of the child's schoolwork or uniform, or show you where they slept. And then we'd discover that the hut, in fact, belonged to their old grandmother, while they lived in a much more comfortable brick house and could conceivably pay for their son or daughter's education themselves. Families would also rent a room in the slums for a month and pretend that they had lived there for ever. It was only through talking to neighbours and the local shopkeepers that the truth would come out. None of them was well off but there are degrees and degrees of poverty and, again, we had to have a cut-off point. Even after we'd done these checks, when the child was on probation at the school we'd go back again, without the child, for one last surprise visit, to make sure everything was as it should be.

We now have a very active Parents' Committee of more than 30 parents who help to verify that the child is poor and from the house the child showed us. Also, whenever I have an unusual disciplinary case or a child's grades are dropping, one of the parents from the Parents' Committee visits the family on behalf of the school to find out if there is a welfare issue behind the child's behaviour. Often enough there is, and those parents visiting families on our behalf really help us run the school. More importantly it helps train these parents to be good leaders and be involved in the school.

The Parents' Committee is also in charge of disciplining fellow parents who are not abiding by the 'Parent Expectations', guidelines that parents have to agree to sign and respect when their child is sponsored. Under the Parent Expectations, parents have to agree to allow their child a couple of hours every night to do their homework and not make the child cart water or herd goats or carry food from the market in all their free time. They have to promise to come into school three times a year to have a ten-minute session with their child's teacher and to pick up their term school report, they have to check the condition of their child's exercise books and textbooks, and they have to wash their child's uniform regularly. Parents also have to make a commitment to help out at regular school working bees, such as planting grass for a new football field or sorting and harvesting the beans and corn, which the school grows for the students and staff to eat.

In those first few months that the school was open, we were changing and refining the criteria for our students all the time. Initially, I'd thought the school would only serve the children of our immediate area, Moshono. I'd imagined that the upper limit of the school would be about 100 children. That seemed to be quite enough to help out locally. I actually turned away a child who lived on the other side of the village church because I thought she lived too far from the school and it would be too tiring for her to walk.

Then a couple of children from Kijenge – just up the road, on the way to Arusha – came and passed the Friday test with flying colours. One of them was Alex Elifas, who was so clearly intelligent that it would have been a crime not to give him the chance of a good education. Then there was a great girl from Kimandolu. We couldn't knock these children back just because it was difficult to go and pick them up. Then we discovered a few kids from Unga Limited – a dirt-poor urban slum area on the far side of town named after a flour factory – who were bright and exceptionally poor. Our little blue bus ended up having to pick up children from all directions. The bus route got longer and longer and the poor driver's day started earlier and earlier. I soon realised that the size of the school would only be limited by the size of the need for it – and that need was, and is, bottomless. It was up to us to work out how to support the school's growth.

If we expanded beyond my original estimation of 100 – which looked very likely – we'd certainly need more land. It was something my father had always drummed into me: 'Whatever your dreams, Gem, however big they are, you have to have land to achieve them.'

With that in mind, I let it be known that I was interested in any parcel of land, of whatever size, that was available close to the school. How would we pay for it? Well, we'd work that one out further on down the track.

Soon after the school opened, one of the villagers, Baba Stanley Letara, came to me saying that he had an acre of land for sale behind the school. It was a typical corn farm, surrounded by other corn farms, criss-crossed by village paths and dotted with small compounds of mud huts, scrawny yellow dogs and dusty kids. The soil wasn't great and there was no water. On the plus side, the plot was land-locked, with no road access, rendering it undesirable to the rich escapees from Arusha who were coming out here in increasing numbers to buy their country retreats.

Land deals in Africa have their own unique procedures. Very few farms have surveyors' maps or council deeds showing exactly who owns which plot and where its boundaries lie, so the first thing that needs to be done is to establish exactly what is for sale. A deputation from Baba Stanley's family joined Richard, Baba (Richard's father), me and some neighbours to walk the boundary and confirm that everyone agreed on the land's dimensions. The asking price was 9,000,000 shillings (about $9000) and so the haggling began. Eventually we agreed on 5,000,000 shillings with a downpayment of 20,000 ($20) and the understanding that we'd pay off the rest within six months – trusting that St Jude would find a way.

In these sort of deals, every interested member of the family – parents, children, siblings – has to be a signatory to the contract to avoid recriminations in years to come. Of the eight people who signed this contract, three were illiterate so they squashed their thumbs on the school office inkpad and made their smudged mark that way. I'd hate to see those prints' authenticity contested in a court of law.

The one small problem was that the matriarch of this family – Baba Stanley's mother-in-law – lived way off in Maasai land, many kilometres south of Arusha. Her signature was vital to the deal. Richard, Baba, Baba Stanley and I jumped into a Land Rover and set off to find her. What an amazing woman! Eighty-five years old and still working in the fields, she emerged from a row of beans, covered in dust and squinting from the heat and glare. After the obligatory greetings and gift-giving, Baba Stanley explained the situation and said that with the money the family would receive from the sale he would build her a fine house to replace the shack she lived in. With that settled, we took out the contract and realised we hadn't brought the inkpad. No worries – we broke open a biro and Bibi Grace made her mark with a thumb dipped in biro ink.

Once the deal was sealed, we decided that we'd use the block initially to grow bananas to feed the children. Bananas here are a staple food, not just a fruit. They're used more often as a starchy vegetable and form the basis of stews with meat or beans. Richard organised for the land to be tilled and sent word out to all the villagers that we'd pay 200 shillings to everyone who dug a hole and another 200 for a suitable banana plant to go in it. Within two days we had a banana plantation!

We managed to pay off about three and a half million shillings (about $3500) over the first three months but it wasn't until eighteen months later that the last 100,000 was handed over. To raise money, we asked our existing sponsors and other donors to donate what they could and, slowly, slowly, a few hundred dollars at a time, we managed to raise the money we needed. It was tough but I never regretted it. Five years later, the School of St Jude has bought eleven other small plots of land around Moshono – a jigsaw puzzle of fields that as a non-profit organisation we've had to pull together under one very complicated land title – but there isn't one piece of land I've ever regretted buying. We've needed every square inch of it. My only disappointment in that first deal was that we later discovered Baba Stanley hadn't fulfilled his promise to Bibi Grace. Oh, sure, she got a new house, but it was about five foot square, made of bare bricks and with no amenities, hardly better than the shack she'd originally had. Women can get a raw deal here.

With new land acquired, we were able to continue bringing in new children, safe in the knowledge that we would be able to expand if necessary. I'm sure that despite our best intentions a few children were offered places who probably shouldn't have been, especially in the early days, when our systems weren't as tight. But we'd never remove the kids, as long as the child appreciated the sponsorship and worked hard and tried to improve. And also, sometimes, even though we tried hard to be consistent, it was the ones who didn't fit any rigid criteria who turned out to be some of our most-loved students. No matter how hard-headed we try to be, this is a very human operation – we're dealing not with machines but with children and all their beautiful, quirky imperfections.

During our earliest Friday testings, there was one boy named Pius who seemed bright and sparky but kept failing the test. This went on week after week until I said to him: 'Pius, you're not going to get into the school unless you do some study. Go home and learn your times tables and do some more reading and then come back and do the test again.'

He was very respectful and didn't look me in the eye, but all the same he said: 'No, Mama.'

'What do you mean, no?' I asked.

'You give me the test again, now. I can do it.'

I said: 'Pius, you've already failed and in any case, now that I look at you, you're way too old to go into Standard 1. How old are you?'

'Eight years old, Mrs Richard.' He was so not eight. He looked about ten. 'Here is my baptism certificate.' This was when the school had just started, before I'd twigged that families were bribing people in authority to produce fake documents. I looked at the document and worked out that, yes, he would be about eight.

'Hmmm, is this yours? Tell me about your family.' Often you can catch them out by asking about their brothers and sisters. Pius had many brothers and sisters and he ran through them saying, this one's 26 and that one's 22. Then he got down to his sister Carolyn: 'And she's eight.'

'Ah ha!' I cried. 'How can she be eight if you are eight?'

Quick as a flash he replied: 'Because we're twins.'

After that I checked out his family and they were so poor but such a lovely family that we let Pius into the school. Around the same time, I had an email from my old boarding school friend Leasa from Cootamundra saying that she'd like to sponsor a child at the school. I replied to her: 'Have I got a doozy for you!' and she's sponsored Pius ever since, at a cost of $1100 a year.

Pius became one of my favourite kids, even though he was always a foot taller than everyone else. I often joked with him that he'd have his own family before he finished school. But sometimes, those are the children you need, the ones with a bit of attitude, which often in the end will get them further than pure brain power alone.

Probably about 20 percent of our children fell into that category – they mightn't have been as strong academically but they were persistent. Another of our extra-persistent ones was little Erick Lucas. He kept coming back Friday after Friday and failing the test, then he took to just hanging around outside the office.

'Erick', I said. 'The test's on Friday. Come back then.'

'But I've got nothing to do,' he said. 'Can't I just sit here and watch?'

After about a week of Erick staying at the school all day, I handed him a bucket of chalk, saying: 'Well, if you're going to hang around, you might as well make yourself useful.'

So every day, Erick's task was to go round the classrooms and hand out chalk to the teachers, a job he took very seriously. Within a week I'd given him a uniform and enrolled him as a student and he did brilliantly. He is still doing the same job to this day, though he now has another student, Innocent Felix, to help him.

Before our program was widely known, we had to fight to get some of these children. Locally, there was a bit of suspicion that we were going to be yet another well-meaning fly-by-night operation, here one moment and gone the next. It's something we have had to struggle against because there are a lot of NGOs (Non-Governmental Organisations) who start out here with the best of intentions then lose heart and eventually leave.

Disinformation campaigns led by a couple of the neighbouring school principals didn't help either.

One of them actually sent home a letter to parents saying that they had information that St Jude's would only sponsor their child for one year and, if they gave up their place at the government school, they wouldn't be able to go back when they'd been dumped by St Jude's. We lost four children because of that particular rumour. It was a lesson to me that we were dealing with ignorant parents who could easily be swayed by misinformation and village talk. Our parents were largely uneducated themselves, so they were unfamiliar with and even suspicious of a school environment. Getting them involved in their children's education would be a challenge but was essential.

I decided to address the parents directly. Gathering them together, I said that I'd heard the rumours going around and knew that some of them were anxious about their children's future. 'I want to promise to you now that we are here for the long term. By the end of the year we will be building more classrooms. We will be buying more buses. Even if something happens so that your child's sponsor can no longer pay their fees, even if the sponsor dies, your child will never lose their place at the school, as long as they work hard and appreciate the support that's been given to them.

'You have to realise that you are the lucky ones whose children have been given a place at the school. There are many – and there will be more – whose children were rejected so of course they're not going to be happy and are going to try to run us down. Just don't listen to it. If you hear anything strange, always come directly to me and I'll tell you the truth.'

After some muttering and talking among themselves, the parents thanked me and left. No more children left the school. Now after a few years the school has proven itself locally and I believe people trust we are going to be around for many, many years to come.

It would be nice to think that was the last of that sort of problem – where ignorant talk caused difficulties in the school community – but of course it wasn't. Yet it did help the parents realise we were all in it together and eventually these same parents – this assortment of illiterate vegetable-growers and maize-sellers – proved to be one of the school's greatest strengths.

Chapter Eight

In March 2002, St Jude sent me exactly what I needed to help me run the developing school: a volunteer called Kim Saville. She intended to come for three months and ended up staying for two years, becoming the backbone of the school. Kim was a Sydney girl but she had been visiting her mother who lived in Armidale – my old area – and was recuperating from an operation. When Kim's mother told her about the school, Kim emailed me, saying, 'I'm not a teacher but if you can use a pair of hands and half a brain, you've got me.'

Kim was exactly the sort of person I needed. When I first saw her, I might have had a moment's misgiving – she's very beautiful and, God knows, this is no place for princesses – but that thought was knocked down pretty quickly. Kim had done a bit of everything – acting, writing, casting, even managing the tall ship the *Bounty* – no job too big, too small, too mucky or too difficult. That's what we needed at the school, people who could turn their hand to anything. Someone who would say, 'Oh no, I'm only here to teach, I couldn't possibly dig a trench' would be no use to me or to the kids.

Kim's first job was to fire our one local teacher who'd been having great difficulties teaching the children. I briefed her on what to say: 'Tell her that we cannot have her here anymore.'

'Hmmm,' Kim said, and wrote a politely worded letter that couldn't possibly cause offence. That teacher was also our next-door neighbour and her mother had a reputation locally for black magic so we didn't want to stir up any ill-feeling. I'd only employed the girl because we'd been a bit desperate and her mother had kept pestering me, showering me with vegetables and fruit, saying that her daughter was an excellent teacher. She had no teaching qualifications but at least her English had been good and she'd been educated to the end of secondary school. However, she really couldn't teach – she aimed too high for our little kinders and Standard 1s and they had no idea what she was teaching them – so Kim had to let her go gently. A few weeks later, her mother sent us a bunch of bananas and Kim was about to eat one.

'Don't eat it!' Ange and I shrieked together. We thought there might be a hex on them or that they could be poisoned, which is a bit silly I suppose. I'm sure they were fine. Almost sure.

But that was one of Kim's great roles here – diplomacy. I tended to run at things like a bull at a gate and she would follow up, mending that gate and smoothing ruffled feathers. I often said that we should have Kim's lipstick in the St Jude's budget, she was so good at schmoozing. She complemented me perfectly. The day after she arrived, the school inspectors were coming to rate the school to check whether it was worthy of registration – and the main inspector was a man in his fifties who even now still asks me about Kim. Unfortunately, on the same day as the proposed inspection I had finally been given a long-awaited appointment to see the Archbishop of Arusha. I was hoping he was going to be able to help us with our volunteers' visas by allowing us to declare ourselves missionaries, which would bypass normal immigration requirements and reduce the cost of our work permits to a fraction of the ordinary amount.

So Kim had suddenly to be the boss for the day and impress the Department of Education inspectors. 'You'll be fine – just make them feel special,' I called over my shoulder as I headed for the car.

'Wait, Gemma, is there anything I should *not* tell them, is there anything I *should*? What should I call them? Your honour? Your most excellentness?'

'Just say "*shikamoo*" – it means I am beneath your feet. And don't go near the back toilets – there's no water.'

Poor Kim. Jetlagged and left to her own resources, all she could remember was that there was an 'm' in what she was supposed to say. Three department officials drove up and Kim came out to greet them with a big smile and hands outstretched. '*Mambo!*' she cried, which would be the equivalent of yelling out 'G'day!' In a country which sets so much store by respect, she was definitely off to the wrong start.

But of course, she fed them tea and cake and flirted with the head inspector and we were granted our school registration. And I did my bit with the bishop and they agreed to help us with volunteers' work visas so everything was fine.

The best thing about that time was the three of us working together: Kim, Ange and me. After a while we could communicate without even speaking. If any of us walked into the office and saw something that needed to be done, we'd do it – there was no line marking where one of our jobs finished and another's started. We meshed beautifully, even though Ange was not even 20, Kim was close to 50 and I was somewhere in the middle and with a new baby. All of us were very hands-on and practical and we didn't wait around.

Like when we dug the trench for the new water pipe. Because my father-in-law was the village chairman, we were allowed to have a direct line to the village pipe, instead of it travelling through four other families before it trickled on to us. We hired the local water *fundi* to lay the pipe. He'd been working for the government water supplier for more than 30 years and looked about a million years old so we figured he'd know a thing or two about plumbing. He arrived with a few boys and they started digging. They dug down about two foot and then made a trench of the same depth along to our yard. With a great show of efficiency and slapping of backs, they laid the pipe, attached it to the mains, and waited. Nothing happened. Not a trickle.

'Hang on a sec,' I said. I remembered watching Dad laying polythene pipes back home. 'You know that water is supposed to go downhill, don't you?' There was some disbelieving muttering. 'This trench is flat. Look! Look at this spirit level. There needs to be a slope.' More muttering and head-shaking. 'Oh, for God's sake!' I said. 'Ange, Kim, let's get some shovels and do it ourselves.'

This was even more entertaining. A small crowd gathered to watch the crazy Western women dig a ditch, talking among themselves and offering helpful advice. Two days of hand-blistering, back-breaking work later, we'd dug a trench that sloped down to a good five feet. By the time we'd reached the tank in the yard, we were all down standing in the trench, which was now well over our heads. Of course the Africans thought it was hilarious. They couldn't see why these idiot women had to build some sort of underground tunnel when all we wanted was to lay a pipe. When we reached the tank, it was past nine o'clock at night. We had torches to light our way in the pitch black and were absolutely filthy. But the pipe worked. The tank was placed about ten feet underground, where water trickles in 24 hours a

Monica Hart (above, in the red shirt) led a Rotary volunteer team that visited the school in March 2002 and built playground equipment for the children. She is now the school's Australian contact, and we couldn't function without her.

After spending two days digging a trench for the school's water pipes, Angela, Kim and I were a mess!

The whole school celebrated the arrival of our first bus, donated by Peter Doherty.

As our first two-storey building was being constructed, Kim and I quickly realised that the beams for the roof were lopsided, so we set about pulling them apart.

My brother Paddy helped teach our local builders so the first two-storey building at the school could be completed.

Parents help sort the school's kidney bean and corn harvest so that their kids can eat at the school every day.

Tom and Judy Wagner with the little blue bus Tom drove for us when our driver was unavailable.

Mum works her magic on my son Jackob during my two-month stay in Australia in 2004.

Toto Fundi (left) was our first carpenter and is still making every door, window frame and roof truss in the school. Amani (right), our young electrician, has grown up along with the school and is indispensable.

David Steller (centre) and his wife, Kerry, lead a Rotary volunteer team that helped to put the roof on a classroom block in 2004.

Edina Emmanuel, one of our very first sponsored students, helps shift
books from a shipping container to the new library, 2004.

ane Kennedy, a marvellous volunteer ibrarian, spent most of 2004 sorting, cataloguing and shelving over 10,000 donated books to create our library.

Students visit the local national parks as a part of the school curriculum and also as reward for good work.

'or five months of the year, crowds like this one gather at the school gates at unchtime every Friday, waiting to take the entrance tests. Less than 20 of these hildren will pass and gain a place at the school.

Before and after. Those lucky students who pass the aptitude and poverty tests are given a uniform, enrolled in the school and then a sponsor is sought from somewhere in the world to support their education.

The moment of absolute happiness when a parent sees their child in a School of St Jude uniform for the first time makes all the days of hard work worth it.

There is a constant flow of sponsors coming to Africa to meet their sponsored children. Here student Margreth Philipo presents her sponsor, Suzanne Kavanagh, Deputy of St Vincent's College in Sydney, with a chicken. Suzanne has twice visited the school with groups of students eager to help out.

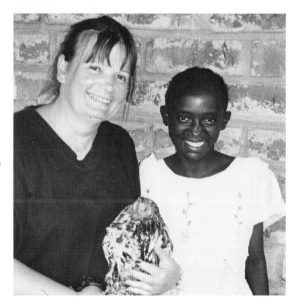

We encourage our visitors to immerse themselves in the local culture. Here Lloyd and Norma Fleming (who have helped send each shipping container we've ever received) enjoy the famous goat barbecue at a local Maasai market.

When Bruce, Cindy, Helen and Gordon Smith visited the school, the staff and students presented them with the traditional gift of thanks! The Smiths have offered the school a great deal of advice, love and support.

Don and Ailsa Hay, former Rotary district governors, sponsored one of the very first students here and ever since have done everything in their power to spread the word about the school.

It is thanks to Rotarians such as Ian Yarker and Jean Tregurtha (left), and Heather Yarker and John Tregurtha (right), that I have had the chance to talk at so many Rotary conferences around Australia and gain support for the school.

Every day, a hot lunch is served in the Laurie Breen Memorial School Hall. To this day lunch has never been late, thanks to all the hardworking cooks and their assistants.

Josephine (far right) started cooking morning tea for us in 2002, and now manages over 20 cooks and cleaners while feeding over 700 hungry mouths each day.

All students learn computer skills from their first day at school.

Baba and Mama, my in-laws, are always there for me if I have a problem or need some advice about the local community. There is no way I could have got the school off the ground had it not been for my Tanzanian family.

Two of the most wonderful women associated with the school are Bibi Anna (left), the head of the Parents Committee, and Bibi Hans (right), the chairman of the school board.

Loma (centre, in the red shirt) leads our wonderful team of bus drivers. There is no government transport to get the kids and staff to and from school, so we have had to provide our own.

The 50-metre long library is a hub of activity all throughout the day.

These gorgeous children are well on their way to a bright future. Back row (from left): Esuvat, Pius, Alex and Athumani. Centre row (from left): Jesca, Erick, Peter (who is the youngest in the school) and Cecilia. Front row: Eliudi.

We could not achieve such wonderful results without the dedication and hard work of the academic leaders. Standing (from left): Nick (Computers), Koringo (Maths), Sister Wanyaga (Religion, Art, Music and Library), Nestory (academic master of the school, on the swing), Diana (Kiswahili), Sebastian (Social Studies), Belinda (Science), Peter (deputy), Didas (English), Coletha (head of the Junior school) and Husna (assistant academic head). In front (from left): Ben (deputy), George and Rasul (assistant heads of departments).

Gone are the days of being alone in the office! Standing (from left): Zac, Baraka, Lucy, Jo, Arianne and my true mate Kim, who helps me run the school. Sitting on the slide (from left): Shweta, Maria, Simon, Mary, Dan and Lulua. In front (from left): Charlotte (bursar), Karin (head of sponsorship) and Di.

Every day I give thanks for the three most important men in my life. Jackob, Richard and Nathaniel forever keep my life full of laughter, love and entertainment!

day, before being pumped up to our big storage tank, and it was enough for all the needs of the school at that time. We have used it as a major water source ever since.

I'm sure Nathaniel has such an easygoing nature because there were so many different people around when he was a little baby. If he had a full tummy and a clean nappy he'd go happily to anyone. But that's the way in Africa – children are brought up by a whole community, not just one mother or father. A good example was that first night Kim arrived, when she met us out at a local restaurant.

'What a pity Nathaniel's in bed,' she said. 'I would have loved to have met him.'

'Oh, no, he's here somewhere,' I said vaguely, gesturing at the crowded restaurant. 'Some lady came up and asked me if she could take my baby to show her family. I think maybe he might be in the kitchen.' Kim looked a little surprised but was prepared to roll with it. It's a bit of an insult to say 'no' to someone who wants to give your child a cuddle or take them home so their family can all see him.

Soon after Kim arrived, we took Nathaniel to the Maasai markets at Monduli. They are huge, sprawling markets, covering the area of about 20 football fields, and they're dusty and chaotic but great. As soon as we got out of the car, all the ancient Maasai crones gathered around Nathaniel, claiming him as a Maasai baby, and off he went, happily sucking on their beaded necklaces, while Kim muttered dark comments about dysentery and other disgusting diseases.

Kim and I shopped a little and had a bit of lunch. The Maasai would bring their goats in to slaughter at the Monduli markets. Lunch meant just going up and choosing a leg for them to roast for you. It was very primitive but delicious. After a couple of hours of pottering, we thought we'd better get going.

'Right ho,' I said to Kim, 'I'll just go and find Nathaniel.' I looked around. The markets stretched in every direction as far as I could see. Every person had uniformly black hair and chocolate skin and there were babies and children everywhere. Even though Nathaniel was a shade or two paler than some of the local children, he was still a little brown baby, blending into a sea of brown people. But I didn't need to worry. He hadn't gone far from where we'd last seen him and was sitting on the lap of an ancient grandmother – who was probably all of 40 – chewing on a strip of roasted goat. He couldn't have been happier or better looked after.

There's a tradition with the Maasai that when they see a baby for the first time, they spit on it for luck. It had come as a bit of a surprise to me when our *askari*, or gatekeeper, pulled back the little blanket wrapping Nathaniel and hoiked in his face. Ange had practically pushed poor Clamian away, without him knowing how he'd offended her. Here he was thinking, *I've just given you a great honour, this is a Maasai blessing*, and then his favour was rewarded by a mad Western woman shrieking at him. But by the time we went to Monduli, I was used to this particular Maasai custom, which was nice because Nathaniel was much blessed.

On the way back from Monduli, Kim and I remembered that we had to stop in at the Kijenge Catholic Church. My old friend Father Chuvi had some new helpers for the outstations in the form of newly ordained priests and there was a celebration which we had been asked to attend. It was late, we were filthy after the markets and Nathaniel was tired. It was the last thing I wanted to do but we thought we'd just pop quickly in, do the right thing, shake a few hands and leave. But, this being Africa, even though we were an hour and a half late, we were still the first people there. By the time all the nuns and priests had arrived, we realised that we were trapped, our car parked in by other cars, and we resigned ourselves to a long afternoon of speeches.

Being the only *wazungu* – white people – at the function, we were seated at the official table with a group of Congolese nuns and priests. Having a baby with you is a great ice-breaker and soon Nathaniel was being passed from nun to nun to priest to nun, being cuddled and tickled and cooed over. He was sucking on crosses and rosary beads and having a lovely time.

Then I noticed after a while that the nuns weren't quite as keen to hang onto the baby anymore. The game of pass the parcel had become more like a game of hot potato, as each pristinely dressed nun passed Nathaniel quickly on to the next. When he came round to me I realised what the problem was. He had done the most abominable poo, right up his back and all over his shirt. Normally no one would mind – in Africa it's supposed to be good luck if a baby poos on you – but they were all in their beautiful white habits for the ordination.

With a sinking sensation, I remembered that I was out of nappies and, being parked in, had no way of nicking out and buying any more in town. Kim spotted what was up. 'Grab some napkins,' she hissed. We started discreetly gathering all the napkins we could from the table, smiling and trying to look unconcerned. I grabbed Nathaniel and a big handful of napkins and bundled him out to the car.

It was only on the way home after the long day that Kim said: 'That was all okay, then. Did you find a nappy in the car in the end?'

'Oh no,' I answered. 'I just whipped my knickers off and padded them out with the napkins and tied them on Nathaniel with a knot. It worked fine. The only thing was,' I said, starting to snort with laughter, 'it was a bit difficult because there were

about 58 kids gathered round the car watching the whole operation so I had to be a little sneaky.' The actions of *wazungu* were
always good for a stare and a giggle, but a white woman taking off
her underpants in public and putting them on a baby? Well that
was really a story worth taking home.

Slowly, slowly, the school was taking a recognisable shape. Three
children had become 10, had grown to 15, to 20. We'd employed
another local teacher for one classroom and Ange took the other
little ones. But financially, we were only just getting by. All three
of us – Kim, Ange and I – had maxed our credit cards paying
teachers and builders and most months we were down to a couple
of dollars in the school account. The only way we had been able
to do the plumbing work and buy the water tanks was because
Chloe Chick, a friend of mine, did a fundraiser in Sydney's
Balmain and made $10,000, which was incredible. Our support
back in Australia was growing all the time.

The difficult thing was that while we were thrilled if a few
more people contacted us, wanting to sponsor a child, we then
had to find places for those children. For every 25 new children,
it meant a new classroom would have to be built, a new teacher
found, and a new school bus bought as there was no public transport for students in East Africa. Growth brought with it its own
challenges but also its own rewards.

A third Rotary volunteer team also came out in March 2002.
The team was led by the now Australian coordinator for the
School of St Jude, Monica Hart, from the Central Coast north of
Sydney. They did an amazing job building a lovely wooden fort
and swings for the kids. I'd initially asked Monica to be the
Australian contact for the school when I moved to Tanzania in
mid-2001. I told her it would only be a matter of a few phone

calls a week and that she definitely would not have to deal with money. Things soon changed and these days Monica works at least five hours a day for the school, taking enquiries and dealing with donations. We wouldn't be able to function without her.

When the next school year began in January 2003, I could see the school that I'd dreamed of emerging. We now had 100 children. One hundred children, who otherwise would have had no future beyond merely trying to survive, now turned up each day and were making huge progress in English and Maths, Kiswahili and Computers. Our first little children were now entering Standard 2 and you could see their confidence growing day by day. At morning tea and lunch time, they kicked balls about and swung on swings, like carefree children everywhere, a far cry from their home lives of chores and responsibilities. When you greeted them, they'd look you in the eye and speak to you in clear, careful English. It was all coming together.

Our curriculum was coming together too. When we first started, we decided not to register ourselves as a government school so as to retain more independence. But we still needed to follow the local curriculum and be registered as a Tanzanian school so that our children would be able one day to go to an East African University. The problem was, we hadn't known exactly what that was. We'd initially had a pile of curricula from Australia which we'd just cobbled together with some extra material we'd found locally. The local education offices did not give us clear rules and syllabi, so it wasn't until late 2002 that we'd discovered on our own that we could buy books which vaguely covered the Tanzanian government curriculum from everyday bookshops here.

So now we had the official curriculum, a slender book each for English, Kiswahili, Science, Social Studies and Maths, and then a shared one for Art, Music and PE. Even with our limited experience, we knew that these would only cover the bare minimum of what our students would need to take them beyond the level of local government education. We began a process of rewriting and expanding on the local texts, a process which has led to our current curriculum, which covers the government requirements but goes further and deeper, especially in the key areas of English and Computers. Due to the lack of good text and teacher resource books our more experienced local teachers have started to write their own textbook-type teacher resource books using their notes, lesson plans and experience from their many years of teaching. Our school curriculum is eternally evolving as we become more experienced with the Tanzanian curriculum.

Another good thing about our expansion was that I was able to employ some more local people to help in different areas of the school, both as teachers and as non-academic support. First there was my sister-in-law Josephine. Josephine was married to Richard's little brother Godfrey and they were really struggling financially. As soon as the school opened in 2002, Josephine had asked me to consider her for any openings as a cook or a cleaner but at that stage, with only a handful of children, we couldn't afford the luxury. However, now in 2003 we needed someone to clean the office and the classrooms. As well, we thought, it would boost everyone's – staff and students – spirits and energy to have a proper morning tea each day. So Josephine was put in charge of cleaning and cooking morning tea. To begin with, she was just a shy, local village girl with no English, who had never worked outside the home and with very little education. But soon she was in charge of a second cleaner, then a couple more cooks.

Now, Josephine heads a team of eighteen cooks and cleaners. It's a massive job, feeding 700-plus students and staff members. She organises all the rosters and orders the huge quantities of food needed. (A typical shopping list might read: six bags of corn,

36 boxes of biscuits, 620 kg rice, 200 kg sugar, 400 kg flour. And that's just the dry goods.) She also coordinates the cleaning not only of the classrooms but also the library, offices, hall, computer labs, staff, science and art rooms and more than 40 volunteer and visitor units. Of course there have been a few problems on the way, but as the role has grown so has Josephine, and now she's confident and flourishing, on a decent salary and building a house for her family. I love that – it makes me think about how connected St Jude's is to the wider community and the role it plays in fostering growth and development, not just of the children, but everyone we work with.

In a very different area of the school – though no less vital – we employed a young local man straight from a computer course to come and teach our children computer skills. Nick didn't have much experience but he was very keen and bright and as our technical capabilities here have grown, so have his role and skills. When, in September 2004, we were donated an Internet account for the school – providing we had it connected – Nick worked on installing the tower and setting up our network. Now, Nick runs everything to do with our computers and is in charge of eight or nine computer teachers and technicians – both Western and local – and all our hardware and software. He's still studying, still learning and has grown so much in confidence and maturity.

Also in early 2003 a young local man called Loma came to drive one of our buses. He was quiet to the point of sullenness, with very little English, but he was a good driver. Again, the job we initially employed him to do was fairly straightforward, but as numbers grew so did his role increase in complexity. The more children we had, the more buses we needed and those buses were required to cover more and more runs: not just the normal school runs, but after-school clubs, excursions, parents coming for meetings, visitors' and volunteers' needs. Loma had to learn to coordinate all these comings and goings on more than fifteen school buses and to ensure – with Richard – that the buses were well-maintained and full of diesel. He also started helping Richard with all the complicated bureaucratic arrangements with the TRA (Tanzanian Roads Authority) that attended the purchase of each new bus. In all this, Loma showed himself to be someone I could really rely on and a leader of others.

As he expanded in his work, we started to see glimpses of his real personality underneath his reserved exterior. Loma is a lovely, warm, friendly man, with a surprising sense of humour. He really came out of himself at a staff party and proved himself the undisputed pool champion of St Jude's.

It's been great seeing my trust and confidence in these three people repaid so fully and to realise that most people, given the right encouragement and support, can rise to meet any challenges. Helping adults realise their potential is just as important as helping children – in some ways, even more so, because adults often have fewer opportunities for growth – and it's a wonderful, ongoing part of our work at St Jude's. As the mission of the school is to train the local people how to run good schools, and more than 40 of the 50-plus academic staff are local, we have to have a lot of on-the-job training especially for the heads of departments and deputies, who are all local people.

Apart from these key local people, we were very lucky in that second year to have another naturally gifted young teacher from Australia who came out to volunteer for the whole of 2003. Edwina Hammond had come out from Sydney a couple of months before the school started with a girl I'd known from my home town. It was just before I had Nathaniel. I was sitting at my old pedal sewing machine, sewing little baby things in the sunshine, and Edwina said to me, 'By the way, I'm going to come back here when the school's open to teach for a year.' Her friend had said, 'Don't raise Gemma's hopes if you don't mean it, Ed,' but she swore that she did.

I didn't take it too seriously – it's a huge call for a young girl to devote a year of her life to working without pay – but, like Ange, she hadn't promised anything she couldn't fulfil. Edwina worked for a year back in Australia to raise the money for flights and living expenses for a year – at that stage we only paid local staff – and came over to teach our Standard 2s.

With our ever-increasing enrolments, our little blue bus had become dangerously crowded and was already travelling about four hours, three times a day. Many other children were walking for as much as two and a half hours a day to get to school. But to buy another bus would cost us around $10,000. While we were receiving donations in bits and pieces, they fell well short of that figure.

Then, out of the blue, I received a letter from a man called Peter Doherty, a Coffs Harbour property developer who had been a great supporter since the early deposit book days. In it he said something like, 'I thought you could use a bit of help, so here's a cheque for $10,000. Do what you like with it.'

I have to say that we went completely wild. What a St Jude's moment! We were all in tears about his unexpected generosity. We called the school together and I told them: 'Thanks to a kind man in Australia, we can buy a new bus! All of you will be able to catch a bus home and you won't be squashed anymore.'

They all clapped politely, but when I brought out a cake and some donuts, they let out an almighty cheer. The whole school celebrated. At the same time, I felt a renewed sense of responsibility to the people who work so hard to send money over to help these children they've never met. We'd never been profligate but we redoubled our efforts to scrimp and save. We used and reused pieces of paper until there wasn't a millimetre left to scribble on and wore pencils down to the very last stub. Even though we'd received a container full of books and pencils before the school opened, we were very aware we couldn't take it for granted that we would receive anything else.

By the end of the previous year – 2002 – we had realised that it wasn't only the buses that were going to be a problem: the first classrooms we'd built would not be able to contain the school's growth for much longer. After getting a local architect to draw up some plans for a simple double-storey building, we had started on a second big block of classrooms, which we planned to later extend with a two-storey library. Rotary had again helped by sending over a team of willing volunteers but we needed to keep building with a local team. With the models of our existing buildings to follow, how hard could it be? Well, quite hard, actually. As with all our work at the school, I was at the bottom of a steep learning curve. Sometimes I think I still am.

First I needed to find a good head brickie. Whenever you wanted to employ someone, there was no shortage of candidates. None of them had any qualifications, mind you, but they were plentiful and willing.

'Wait, Mama, I know a very good brick *fundi*,' one of the blokes who worked at the school cried and dashed off to the village. He returned with another young man who looked suspiciously like a close relative.

'Can you build a brick wall?' I asked.

'Oh yes, Mama, of course, not a problem. Brick walls? Psssh, easy.'

'Thank God for that,' I said. We set him and his team to work and I returned to my paperwork in the office. A few hours later, I heard a shriek from Kim:

'F***, Gem, have you seen the brickwork?'

I raced outside. A handful of guys were hard at work with a lot of bricks and cement. Their technique was original: they placed one brick, then covered it with about ten centimetres of mortar, then put another brick directly on top, without overlapping. They had only built the first few rows but the wall was already seriously unstable.

Kim and I looked at each other and, with one mind, raced out and started bashing down the dodgy wall before it set. All these 'brickies' stood around watching, obviously thinking we were completely unhinged. When we'd undone all their morning's work, I called for the brick *fundi*.

'Here, Mama. I spent all morning building that beautiful brick wall,' he said, aggrieved.

'Do you call that a brick wall? Have you ever actually *seen* a brick wall, let alone *built* one?'

'Ahhhh,' he said wisely. 'Now I see. You wanted a brick wall *wazungu* style. Why didn't you tell me?' Well, yes, I did want a Western-style wall, if the alternative was the mess I'd just seen. And so that brick *fundi* was sacked and we had to start from scratch, with one who claimed to be a master of the *wazungu*-style wall.

The building program was always the hardest part of creating the school. Selecting children was the most emotionally draining and difficult but the actual building was the toughest. First, as a young, white woman working in a very patriarchal society, it took a long time to be taken seriously, either by builders or suppliers. I probably went through 300 different builders and after firing the first ten in quick succession, I soon found I was being given a little more respect.

Then there were the suppliers. Not one of them would take our school cheques, which was very frustrating. If I wanted to buy

200 bags of cement, I had to go to the bank, withdraw two million shillings (1000 times 2000 shilling notes) and lug them in a suitcase to the bulk supplier. Then I had to go around to the market to haggle with the truck boys to find one who was prepared – at a price – to load the cement and take it out to the school. Every step of the way was just that much harder than it might have been if it was, for example, my brother setting up the school. But I had to do it myself. If I handed it all over to Richard, I'd never gain their respect.

As I became a more regular customer, the cement supplier unbent, and actually supplied the labour for loading the cement. In time, they even accepted my cheques. Eventually, they allowed me credit when I really needed it. Now I just make a phone call and the cement is brought out and loaded into our store without me lifting a finger. The same goes with the steel suppliers and the hardware shops. It just took a bit of extra time to get there.

Finding the right people to help me was very difficult. If I was in Australia running a school, I would have had a building advisory committee and the difference between builders would be more a matter of who gave the best quote than any real level of skill. Of course, some builders are better than others but they would have all been to school, then had some further training – apprenticeships and TAFE – and would be suitably qualified. Here, I was dealing with people who were unqualified and in most cases would never have completed primary school. Up to this day I am yet to see any building qualification from any of my 50 or more builders. I could have hired outside contractors but they would have charged five times what we could afford. Our builders came from extremely disadvantaged backgrounds and had little hope for the future. No wonder some of them had such short-term goals.

Because St Jude's was constantly expanding, we offered a real future for these guys. If they did their work well, they were guaranteed ongoing employment up until this day and long into the future, and we paid well above the average local wages. You'd think it would be in anyone's best interests to do a good job for us and, at the very least, not to try to cheat or rob us. But that didn't seem to stop some of them. If they could see a way of making a quick dollar by stealing a screwdriver or 'mislaying' a few bags of cement, then they'd do that, even though it put at risk their employment worth hundreds of times that amount.

I realised two things. One was that I would have to personally supervise every bit of building work, from counting the bags of cement to checking that we were receiving the right quality and quantity of bricks. No one else could do it. The second, linked, realisation was that if things went wrong and people stole or abused the system, it was my fault, not theirs. These people had very little in their lives, little materially or educationally and little in the way of ethical learning. If I allowed temptation to come their way and they succumbed, then it was entirely up to me. So I made sure that things were harder to steal – for example I bought tools with noticeable, fluorescent handles – and resolved not to employ middle men. Why put someone in a position where they could be tempted to take a cut for themselves? It was safer – though admittedly it created a lot more work – to do it all myself.

Sometimes, like when we built the water trench or bashed down the brick wall, this meant being more hands-on than perhaps you'd expect in your average school job. Another time, Kim and I were in the office, sending our reports to sponsors to let them know how their children were progressing. With one eye, we were also watching the library being built, which was a big excitement because it was going to be our first ever two-storey building.

Finding builders who could build two storeys was not easy. I think they misunderstood what the purpose of the ground floor was. Actually, who can hazard a guess what they were thinking? I walked onto the site when the wooden formwork for the bottom classrooms had been erected and had to point out that if they continued the way they were building then the roof would be only one and a half metres high. I explained that, while I was not very tall, there were some children – and teachers too – at the school who were already that height and that they'd prefer not to hit their heads on the ceiling.

'But Mama,' they said. 'We only have poles this long, we don't have any that are as big as three metres.'

Moments like that remind you of the level of skills with which you're dealing. When I showed them how they could attach two pieces of wood together to make a pole *double the length*, they were full of admiration. We also had trouble even finding an engineer who was prepared to give approval, for a pittance, to such a radical concept as a two-storey building.

Once we'd got the formwork sorted out, the builders began to lay the beams which would later support the roof. As Kim and I watched, again it became clear that something strange was happening. The beams were sloping dramatically, so that the ceiling at one end of the room would end up a good foot taller than the other. It was pretty obvious that this was happening, because the columns on one side were so much higher than on the other. The two of us watched in silence, beyond puzzlement. Eventually, Kim said: 'I'm sure there's a good reason for that, maybe to store a tank or something . . .' She trailed off.

'I don't THINK so,' I said. 'Come on. Quick!' And we rushed over. The cement was still wet. 'We're going to have to smash it down and redo the slab. Come on!' I climbed up and straddled a beam, Kim following. We grabbed hammers and just smashed away, to the stunned bemusement of the builders. I never did find out what they'd been thinking when they'd decided to give us lopsided ceilings. Nothing, I suspect.

Thank goodness my little brother Paddy came over to help. He taught the builders so many techniques that they still use today. Even though he found it really frustrating at times, his contribution to the school was invaluable. To this date, the builders have repeated that double-storey building five more times, as we have needed more classrooms and accommodation for the school to expand.

Every bit of work was trial and error. Every different person gave you different advice, so in the end you just had to have a go and see what worked. I'd put down a floor but it was only after it was laid that I'd think, *It would be nicer if it were painted*. So I'd paint the floor before realising that paint would just scratch off. The next time we'd put paint into the cement but we'd discover that we'd bought the cheap pooch powder which just sinks to the bottom of the cement and that we should have bought German pooch powder. By the time we built the third set of floors, we knew about the German pooch powder, we mixed it into the cement and it was all lovely. So each time we built something, we became a little more experienced and things ran a little more smoothly.

When Nathaniel was about nine months old, I had discovered that I was pregnant again. It was a bit sooner than I'd intended but I was thrilled. With my family background, I wanted to have quite a few children, though I wasn't expecting to emulate Mum's eight. We were so busy that I didn't have much time to think about the pregnancy, and again worked right up until I went into labour.

It was the same time of day as I'd gone into labour with Nathaniel. Again, I was cooking dinner when I felt the first pains. We rang Dr Kamaro and told him we were going into the hospital but not to worry, we wouldn't need him until the following day.

This time I was prepared. I remembered the cold hard steel of the trolleys and took with me some pillows and blankets from home. It wasn't like my first experience. This time, there were five or so other women in the ward, all in the throes of labour. You could tell by their eyes that they were in pain but they lay almost silently on their beds, with only an occasional groan or roll from side to side. Richard was soon sent packing from the all-female environment by a nurse so he spent the night in the car and I was on my own, with only a pillow to squeeze.

Very early the next morning, when my contractions were becoming much more intense, one of the nurses examined me and told me I still had a long way to go. My body was telling me otherwise.

'Nurse!' I called her back. 'I think I'm going to have the baby soon. Could you please test me again?'

She didn't say it, but her expression was eloquent: *Oh my God. Spare me from these whingeing Western women. You're just having a baby, we've been doing it for a couple of million years.*

'You're a long way off,' she repeated. 'And it's not procedure to test twice within the hour.'

'Well can you call Dr Kamaro for me then?'

'Call Doctor? Certainly not. At this time of morning!' And off she walked.

I didn't have a phone with me so, doubling up every few minutes with contractions, I walked out of the hospital, down the stairs, and into the carpark to find Richard and wake him up. 'Rich, the nurse is being a real witch and I think I'm about to have the baby. Can you ring Dr Kamaro for me?'

'Yes. No. Oh no. I don't have his card with me. I don't know his number.' And poor Richard tore off in a cloud of dust to drive back to Moshono to find Dr Kamaro's number.

Meanwhile I walked back up the stairs and was discovered outside by the nurse.

'What *are* you doing? You'll freeze to death. Come inside,' she said, pulling me back in. Then suddenly she said: '*Now* what are you doing?'

'I don't want to push, but I have to,' I said.

'Oh my goodness, you really *are* having the baby,' she said, and quickly she whipped me onto a table and delivered another fine, healthy boy. Jackob had curly brown hair, big melting brown eyes and Rice dimples, and was utterly gorgeous. I was glad he was smaller than Nathaniel by half a kilo and that it had been an uncomplicated delivery, considering I did it virtually on my own. When Dr Kamaro finally did arrive he told me never again to worry about ringing him, whatever the problem, whenever the time.

Back at home with Jackob, this time I was prepared for the goat soup and the procession of men bearing gifts. One tradition I perhaps should have followed more was that in the weeks following the birth, your mother-in-law is supposed to rub your stomach with hot coconut oil, to make it shrink back to normal. I tried it but it really was hot and I preferred to live with the stomach.

Jackob was born in April 2003 and when he was only three weeks old I had to fly with him and Nathaniel to Australia. Brisbane was hosting the World Rotary Conference and I had been asked to speak at it. It was a tremendous opportunity for me to raise funds and let people know about St Jude's internationally, but the timing could have been better. Since Richard and I could not afford to both go, as only my ticket was being paid for, I was on my own, with a very active eighteen-month-old toddler and a tiny little newborn baby. I'd also left behind a half-finished building project in the care of John, a builder whom I trusted, but only up to a point. I'd had so many disappointments already. At least in this instance, a lot of the hard work had been done by my brother Paddy, who'd been over to supervise some of the building. John, who had worked with Paddy while he was here, just had to finish off the back of the classrooms.

It was the plane trip from hell, so it was heavenly when I arrived – Mum was waiting for me at the airport and everything was all right. Babies and children can melt the hardest of hearts and Mum adored my children from the start. The day after I arrived I had to speak at the conference and she just took over with the children, like a cross between a loving grandmother and the most efficient nanny imaginable. I went from talk to talk and hotel to hotel, and Mum did everything bar the breastfeeding. I have a photograph of us checking into a glamorous hotel that Rotary had arranged. We were all so tired that we were half-draped over the gold luggage trolley we were pushing – and in it was tiny Jackob.

Having children really made me appreciate how wonderful Mum was. We went home to the property, Wyoming, after the conference and I remember one of my brothers and I coming into the kitchen one evening. Mum was cooking Nathaniel's dinner, mashing the potato with Nathaniel sitting happily on the benchtop and Jackob in one arm. I had a glimpse of what her life must have been with all of us children and realised how much I could learn from her, but I just said, 'Gee you're good, Mum.'

With Nathaniel I'd struggled along, not really knowing what I was doing and acting on instinct. But at this crucial time in Jackob's life, for a nice long period I had Mum and Dad to turn to and I realised how wise they were. If Jackob was crying, I'd assume he was hungry and go to feed him, just as I would have done with Nathaniel at the same age. But Dad would say, 'Give him to me, Gem,' and after about 20 minutes of patient patting, Jackob would let out a huge burp and be happy again. In effect, because I had two months in Australia when Jackob was so little, he had more of a regimented, Western babyhood while Nathaniel had had a more unstructured African one.

In Africa, children are never ignored – if they cry they are fed and they're with you day and night. We had tried to have a cot made for Nathaniel when he was a baby but the wood *fundi* had never heard or seen of one before and his first attempt to make the cot was woeful. So Nathaniel slept in our bed, which secretly I loved. But it also meant he didn't sleep through the night for the first six months and I fed him constantly. At home, under Mum's rule, Jackob was immediately put on a strict four-hourly feeding regime and was sleeping through the night within a week or two of arriving in Australia.

Each way had its plusses and minuses, but when I returned home to Africa I was glad Jackob was in such a good sleeping and eating pattern. I couldn't be constantly carrying him around or feeding him because I had to undo a big mess of John the builder's making. The work he had completed was appalling. I'd left him to plaster the back walls of the classrooms squarely, then cover them with pooch powder, the red powder that we use to colour all our plaster work. Instead of plastering, he'd just sprayed the pooch powder directly onto the brickwork. He thought no one would notice what went on at the back of the classroom and was banking on the fact that, in my absence, everybody at the school had taken on extra roles and there was no one who cared enough about what he was doing to oversee it properly.

I was livid. How could he do this to us? How could he be so short-sighted? He'd been a good worker before – why would he throw away a solid future with us for the sake of making a few shillings in the short term? It drove me mad and I still growl every time I see that shoddy work he did.

Then, weirdly, Jackob stopped breastfeeding, aged only four months. At first, I wondered whether it was because I was over-stressed and he could sense it, so I discussed it with Richard.

'You know, Gem,' he said. 'Sometimes a baby goes off its mother's milk when she gets pregnant. What do you reckon?'

'I can't be!' I said, appalled. I'd just been away for two months. I had a toddler, a little baby and a fast-growing school to run. I couldn't possibly fit another baby into our lives at the moment.

But Richard was right – Dr Kamaro confirmed that I was pregnant again. And before I'd had time to assimilate this news and work out how I felt about it, I found out that my dear, dear father had cancer.

CHAPTER NINE

It was September 2003 when the boys rang me up. My brothers are great guys but not known for their reliability as correspondents, so I was immediately on the alert.

'What's up?' I asked.

'It's Dad,' one said. 'He's got cancer. It's in his bladder but they reckon they've got it in time and they can cut it out. We're really sorry to have to tell you, Gem, but we just thought you should know.'

Dad ill. It wasn't something that bore thinking about. Dad was never ill. To get him to the doctor was like pulling teeth. Children are selfish and egocentric, whatever age they are. We like to think that we can leave our parents but that they can't leave us, that we can live on the other side of the world but they will be where we left them forever, dependable and unchanging. Hearing that my big, strong Dad was seriously ill was something I found very difficult, especially as it was a situation in which I was powerless. I'm always fine if I have a plan of action, not so good if I just have to wait.

By all accounts, the operation on his bladder went well and he followed it with a successful course of chemo. He returned quickly to work and, in fact, opened another office in Tamworth while he was ill. His stamina was amazing.

I kept in touch with what was going on with Dad but there was nothing much else I could do. I knew I'd be going home that year for a Wyoming Christmas so I just knuckled down to work. Amid the worry about Dad and the usual dramas and crises of school life, there was a lot that was going well.

Edwina was going to leave at the end of the year. She'd been such an important part of the school for the time she was there and had been so involved with the children that we wanted to make her farewell really special. She'd never been paid and had lived in very basic conditions without complaint. I asked her what she'd like to do to celebrate.

'Do you know what I really want?' she said. 'I'd like to take the children to the fair and for a sleepover at the school.' There was a travelling fair that had come to Arusha for a couple of months, like the sort you see in country towns all over Australia, only with much older rides and dodgier side shows.

The whole night out was a hoot. I don't know who looked more excited, the children or Edwina, when they all arrived to be taken out to a restaurant for chicken and chips. None of the children had ever been in a restaurant before, so it was a very big deal for them even though the restaurant itself was probably the cheapest place in town. It was just a bamboo and bark hut on the side of the road. The extent of the cooking was throwing some chickens on the fire, then pulling them apart and piling them on a plate. Some chips, some salt, and dinner was served.

'Just pace yourself, kids,' we kept saying, to deaf ears. These were children who had to struggle for survival on a daily basis, so how did we think they'd react when confronted with towering plates of chicken pieces? It was quite horrifying to watch, with chicken and chips flying everywhere, all of the children intent on cramming as much food into their mouths as they could fit.

'Are you enjoying yourselves?' I asked, in appalled fascination. No answer, just a dozen heads bobbing and a few quick hand gestures which I interpreted as: 'No time for questions, there's eating to be done.'

Dinner over, we took the children, now shiny with chicken grease, to the fair and gave them each a number of tickets. Again, we warned: 'Just pace yourselves.'

'Yes, Mrs Richard, yes, Miss Edwina,' came the reply on the wind, as they raced off to the flying chairs. One ride and they were ready to go again. Alfani was the first to vomit.

'Sit down, Alfani, and you'll feel better.'

'No, Mrs Richard, I'm better already and I'm going on the Hurricane!'

They blew all their tickets in the first ten minutes, and it would have been all over if some kind stranger hadn't given them an extra bundle, which meant they could all have one more ride each. They chose the Ferris Wheel and set off on their circuit, waving madly. I don't know who started vomiting this time but it set them all off. Yet when they got off the ride they were as happy as anything: 'That was great – can I go on it again?' It was all part of the event for them.

Then we went back to the school and they bundled into the library to watch *The Lion King* for the hundredth time, fascinated by all those African animals that lived in the bush only hours away but that most of them had never had the opportunity to see until they came to the school and were taken there on excursion. It was a perfect send-off for Ed.

Around the same time Edwina left at the end of 2003, I went back to Australia again, this time just with Jackob, for a Wyoming

Christmas. Poor old Nathan was now two – the age at which children have to have their own seat on a plane – and I couldn't afford his fare. NEGS, the school where I'd worked after coming back from my volunteer work in Uganda, had organised my ticket in return for my speaking at their end-of-year Speech Day. It was perfect timing – I wouldn't have been able to come for a last Christmas with Dad without such financial support. I'd almost call that another St Jude's moment.

It was lovely to be home. Dad had lost a lot of weight but was still himself and it was wonderful to have time together. Being pregnant again in Australia was a bit of a treat because everyone kept saying, 'Sit down, Gemma, don't carry that.' Even though I didn't see that all the cosseting was necessary, it made a nice change.

That was a strange, disrupted year for me at the school in 2004. In a way I was divided between all that we were doing at St Jude's and thinking of my father far away, the most important man in my life besides Richard and my sons. It's not that I wasn't fully focussed on my usual business of finding sponsors, placing children, supervising teachers and running the building program, but I did take my hands off the reins a few times because I wanted to spend any time I could with Dad.

I was ill more than once as well. Two or three days after I arrived back from Australia, I started vomiting. I couldn't hold anything down and had a bone-draining exhaustion I couldn't shake. I was diagnosed with malaria – which I came down with fairly regularly – dosed with anti-malarials and sent home. Three weeks later I went to the doctor again, burning with fever. Malaria again. Again, I was given medicine. By this stage I was about five months pregnant and wasn't especially happy to be taking so much medication, but I had no choice. People still die here of malaria – more frequently than of AIDS – and I had two children to think about.

About four days later, I began to have cramps. I tried to tell myself that they didn't mean anything but in my heart I knew it was labour starting. When I went to the bathroom, I saw that I was bleeding and began to cry.

Richard was in town so Ange and Kim laid me down on the bed and went to phone him. I knew I was going to lose the baby. I was getting contractions every five minutes, just as I had when I laboured with the boys. Richard rushed home and quickly took me into hospital but as I walked up the front stairs – the same stairs I went down to see Richard in the carpark when I was having Jackob – I realised that the baby was already emerging. It was the worst thing. Ange and Rich got me up the stairs and into a ward and the nurse delivered the poor little dead five-month-old baby into a kidney dish. Richard was in tears again, but I was strangely numb. Then, just as I was losing it, Dr Kamaro turned up after having driven more than 200 kilometres to be at my side. He said that he needed to clean me up, so he put me under a general anaesthetic and everything went blissfully black.

When I swam back into consciousness, Dr Kamaro was sympathetically looking down at me and saying, in a matter-of-fact voice: 'You understand, Gemma, that you've lost the baby. I've had to give you an anaesthetic. This happens to a lot of women. You're young and strong – you can have another.'

I went home and asked Richard: 'Where's the baby?'

He told me that it is traditional in these circumstances for the grandparents to deal with the baby and that his parents had arranged for a little baptism and burial ceremony. 'But where's it buried?' I asked again.

'My parents won't say, Gemma, and that is the way it is to remain,' said Richard. 'We don't talk about it here. We get over it. Get on with life and looking after the two beautiful boys that we have.' And we never discussed it again. Three years later I would find out that his parents buried the baby in our garden.

It sounds a cold, even inhumane way to deal with such a loss. In some ways it was, but I also understood the reasons behind it. Africans lose so many children, both during pregnancy and in early infancy, that they can't dwell on individual deaths to the extent that we do. They mourn, accept and move on, concentrating on the children they do have, who still need feeding and care. I know that if I'd been in Australia I would have been offered all sorts of counselling or group therapy. Certainly people's sympathy would have reminded me of my grief. In Africa, I just got straight back to work, which helped with the healing process.

Again – the same problems crept up repeatedly at every stage of development – we were at a crisis point with our buses. We needed more than two to cope with ferrying the ever-increasing number of children around. Some children were actually getting hurt on the journey but, as always, we were down to our last few dollars in the bank each month and had no idea where the huge sums needed could come from.

I've always found that St Jude waits until the last moment to help us. There is a statue of him on my desk, next to my always-full 'to do' spike where the builders put their lists of materials that they need me to buy, and he always looks a little bit brown around one side of the head where I give him the odd, friendly whack, just to remind him that we are here. 'C'mon, St Jude,' I say. 'We need you, mate.' But there was no miraculous response or unexpected cheque in the mail this time.

Just as we were feeling a bit desperate, Ange's mother and father came over to visit her. We were living hand to mouth. Ange and Kim had given each other a jar of pickles for Christmas and thought they were really going to town. So when Ange's parents arrived and asked me how they could help, I said: 'Take Ange away for a few days to a nice lodge. Feed her up, give her a good bath and just indulge her for a bit.'

So they took her out of town to a lodge called Rivertrees, where the only thing to disturb the tranquillity is the low voices of waiting staff asking whether you'd like a drink. It was a quiet time of year and there were only two other people staying at the lodge, an American couple in their seventies named Tom and Judy Wagner. They'd lived in Africa in the '60s during the transition to independence and had returned to see what changes had occurred in the intervening years.

The Wagners were a lovely couple who genuinely cared about Africa and its people. Judy is an elegant, warm-hearted but at the same time practical woman. They'd both worked for the government in their time so she must have been quite a powerhouse, but she was still the sort of person who baked her own pies from scratch and Tom was the archetypal gorgeous, generous grandfather. The Wagners and Baileys struck up a friendship, so when Ange's parents mentioned that they were dropping Ange back to the school, the Wagners offered to drive them all over in their hired Land Rover.

It was then that the bus crisis came to a head. Normally, if the bus driver couldn't work, Richard or I could always cover for him. But that day the driver, Joseph, told us he would not able to drive the younger children home on the next day's 12.30 run. Richard was on safari and I had a meeting with the Anglican bishop, who was coming out for lunch and to look at how we made our furniture.

Our saviour came from left field. The Wagners heard about our problem and Tom said, 'Actually, I used to do a lot of driving when I was here in the '60s and I still have a bus licence so I'd be very willing to help out if you'd like me to.'

'Gosh,' I said. 'That would be great. I'll send an adult from the school with the children so she can show you where all the children live.'

So the next day, this genial, silver-haired American gentleman on holidays came over and took on the little blue bus route for the afternoon. It took him four hours to drop all the children home because their homes were all scattered through the district. He returned a little shaken, first by the appalling condition of the roads he had to face, and second by the overcrowding of the little blue bus.

'Don't you think you could do with another bus?' he asked.

'We sure could!' I said, not realising what his intentions were.

'Right,' he said. And when he returned to America, he sent us a cheque for US$10,000, which we used to buy a wonderful new school bus, which now carries many children to and from school.

Now that seemed to me to be a definite St Jude's moment. If Tom Wagner hadn't met Ange's parents, he wouldn't have come out to the school. If we hadn't been unable – the one time in the school's history – to cover for the bus driver, he wouldn't have driven the bus. If he hadn't driven the bus, he wouldn't have known how great our need was. Each event is unlikely in itself and, added together, the whole chain of events is too fortuitous to be attributed to mere coincidence.

Soon after, it was time for the yearly Australian Rotary conferences in March. While I didn't want to leave the family, fundraising is just too vital to the school's wellbeing, so I reluctantly went. It was also an opportunity to see my father, who was frail but in good spirits.

This time, I returned to the school to find nothing but good news. The first thing I saw as I drove in the gates were hordes of kids, bouncing around on a lush green football field. In

January, we'd asked the parents to come in to help us plant the grass on the field and it had been a great project, not least because it helped give the parents pride in and a sense of ownership of the school. I've always been a great believer in reciprocity. The parents of our children mightn't have a lot to give, but if they contribute what they can, then it helps them break free of the hand-out mentality, which ruins anyone's self-motivation.

It's a lot of fun as well. When all the parents come together for planting or harvesting of the kidney beans or maize, there's a lot of banter and we all get to know each other a lot better. It's a huge job, sorting out the beans or threshing the corn kernels, but it goes much more quickly when you have 500 parents helping, and makes them realise we're all part of the community here.

It's not unlike making the children responsible for their personal possessions. We used to have a big problem with kids losing their ties. When they lost a tie, we'd give them a new one and it was costing quite a bit of money. Then we thought we'd try an experiment. 'Anyone who loses their tie or any other item of clothing will have to contribute to the cost of a replacement,' we told them. A few still went on losing theirs but when they realised we were serious and we made them pay a nominal amount – say, $1 for a new tie – amazingly they all managed to hang onto them and we've had few problems since with lost property.

The other fantastic development was that the library was up and running, thanks to the tireless efforts of Jane Kennedy, a volunteer who stayed for most of 2004 to sort, catalogue and shelve over 10,000 donated books. When we'd started the school, I'd just looked at all the books we'd collected and said, 'Yeah, that's about Standard 1 level, that's probably Standard 2.' I'd colour-coded the spines according to the grade level, but our library system hadn't developed into anything more sophisticated.

Jane was wonderfully methodical – and a real unbeliever, especially about my faith in St Jude. I've never minded other people's beliefs or lack of them. It's all meant with a good spirit. Kim hates religious doctrine, Jane was a total cynic, and that's fine with me. Just because I'm a Catholic doesn't mean I expect others to be.

Again, because we'd kept expanding, we were desperate for another bus – I know, it's repetitive, but that's the nature of the beast. Jane and I were travelling home from town, where we'd been for our regular daily session at the Internet café – this was before we had Internet access at the school – and I said to her: 'It's beyond a joke with the buses again. I know you don't believe in it, but at tomorrow's assembly, I'm going to make everyone do a novena to St Jude.'

Jane just looked at me and said, 'Gemmmaaaaa' in a way that made it clear she thought I was deluded.

'You just wait,' I said. 'Before we get to day nine I bet you we will have a donor for a new school bus.'

The next morning, it was our regular Friday assembly. Assemblies are always beautiful. The children start off with the Tanzanian national anthem, and hearing all their voices raised together, singing in Swahili, always brings a prickle to the back of my eyes. Then every day – and in class time on non-assembly days – the children say a prayer to St Jude. They say: 'Glorious Apostle St Jude, helper of those with problems, please listen to us.' And then they are allowed to put their hand up to ask for individual help, perhaps for their sick mother, their sponsor or their dad who's out of work. But this Friday I told the children that for the next nine days, at least one of them had to put their hand up to say to St Jude that we needed a new bus.

On day four, I went into town to check my emails and, surprise, surprise, there was an email from a North Sydney woman called Joy Lambert whom I'd never met before in my life, saying that she was interested in funding a new bus. The first thing I did when I returned to the school was race up to the library.

'Oi, Jane,' I shouted, waving a printout of the email. 'What do you think about St Jude *now*?'

I don't think I ever convinced her, but she was too nice to say so.

In May, Mum and Dad decided they wanted to travel to France. They'd first gone to France more than 40 years before, on their honeymoon. Although she hadn't known it at the time, Mum had already been pregnant with Tim and she always maintains that Tim had such a saintly character because he'd been bathed before birth in the holy waters of Lourdes. So France, and Lourdes in particular, was very special to them and they wanted to go back to where they spent the first weeks of their marriage, to come full circle.

Dad obviously felt that his life was drawing to a close and he told me: 'Your mother and I started our marriage on the road. It would be lovely if we went back and that's where we finished it.' It was to be a sentimental journey. When I heard about their plan, I decided to surprise them so Jackob and I flew out and spent two weeks with them in France. In fact, by this time, Dad seemed much better and was able to wander round the old churches with us and have a few good dinners out. I could return to school with a lighter heart than I'd had for a while.

I don't know what it is with this business – perhaps it's like this whatever you do. But I always seem to be on one side of a seesaw or a set of scales. One side is given a boost – Dad seemed more healthy, we had a new bus for the school – and the other side comes crashing down. Maybe it's more like a game of snakes and ladders: you happily climb a ladder and don't realise that a snake's waiting in the next square to drag you back down a few rows.

For years we'd had a family of wonderful Maasai boys from Monduli working as our security guards. Theft is a big problem around here. With so much computer and office equipment and often large amounts of cash for paying builders on the premises, there would be no way we could function without adequate security. Because it's so important to the Maasai to acquire and keep as many cattle as possible, from the earliest age little Maasai boys are trained to stay up all night to watch out for raids on their herd by lions or other unscrupulous Maasai. So around Arusha, it's common knowledge that if you need a good security guard, especially a night watchman, then find yourself a Maasai. The boys we'd been using were a family of brothers, all from the same father but different mothers, and they were all excellent.

Then I was approached by another Maasai boy named Emmanuel, from a different family. He too was looking for security work. I knew his father from town and he was a man I liked and respected so I was happy to give his son a go.

It was June and the builders were due for their monthly pay. I had quite a few builders at the time. Our latest project was yet another classroom block, to keep up with the ever-increasing number of children being sponsored. This one would house twelve classrooms over two storeys. It was our most ambitious program to date and I'd searched hard for some top-class people to help us.

On the way out from Kijenge, I'd noticed a house which had been newly built for some people who were working with the Rwanda war crimes tribunal at the UN. Three storeys high, its column work was beautiful. *That's the sort of work we need*, I'd thought.

So I'd gone to the builders, found out who their foreman was

– a nice, professional bloke called Julius – and offered him a job, paying about double the local going rate. Of course he'd been delighted to take it.

'Rich,' I'd said that night. 'I think we've cracked it. We've got such a good foreman this time.'

'Just wait, Gemma,' he'd said. 'Remember this is Tanzania. He'll be good for two weeks and then you'll be coming back to me with a different story. Just don't tell him how good you think he is or he'll take advantage of you.'

But the next couple of months proved Richard wrong. Julius was fantastic. His work was beautiful, and things were proceeding to schedule. It meant I could spend more time in the office – even occasionally with my family – and not on the building site. It was such a relief.

We sent a volunteer into the bank to bring us back US$6000 in cash, as progress payments for a building job and also for the June 2004 salaries. We distributed some of it and then I left the rest on a shelf in my locked office overnight, ready as usual for the school bursar to give to all the local staff the next day.

In the morning, I came in and looked for the bundle of notes. Not there. The only clue that anything had been disturbed was a flurry of leaves on my desk and computer, clearly brought in from the tree that had provided the thief a way in via the roof. It was the only way anyone could have entered the building.

We had a group of NEGS students and teachers from Australia over at the time camping on the grass outside the office. We had dogs who would set up a racket the moment they sniffed someone unfamiliar coming by at night. If the thieves had been in any way professional, they would have taken my very valuable camera, or some of the computer equipment which was standing around, unprotected. But they'd taken only the money and had known exactly where to find that.

Our new guard Emmanuel and his friend Peter had been working that night. It had to be them. Of course, reporting the theft, and the subsequent police investigation, was a comedy of errors. We went into town and made a report, which was then lost and had to be redone. The thieves had left clear finger-prints on the roof which the police sent down to Dar Es Salaam where, obviously, they disappeared and were never heard of again.

But I wasn't willing to sit back and wait for it all to go away. One of the things I've found here, particularly being a woman, is that I have to prove at every point that I'm here for the long haul, I won't be taken advantage of and I won't go away. I insisted on prosecuting those boys. Some two years later, we were finally able to present our statements in court, but on the rare days that the judge was there, the police prosecutor was on holidays; if they were both there, the boys weren't available. Not long after, Peter was caught red-handed committing another theft and jailed. I said to the police: 'If the system was a little bit more efficient, Peter wouldn't have had that second opportunity to steal because he would have already been behind bars.'

Anyway, it was a bit disheartening but it was only one incident and 2 staff members out of 150. No one was killed, no one was hurt. It was just money, so we moved on.

Not long after Mum and Dad had returned home from Europe, Dad started suffering chronic back pain. He'd always had a few problems with his back, ever since years ago when he had moved a big semi-trailer-load of sheep from Guyra down the 'Devil's Pinch', a notorious stretch of the New England Highway. The truck's brakes failed and Dad ended up having to roll the big semi on the highway down the gully to stop. Most of the sheep were killed and Dad almost broke his back. In about August 2004, the back pain returned but was dramatically worse, so Dad went back to his oncologist and heard the news we'd been dreading. The cancer had now spread to his back bone.

Amazingly, through all this Dad was still working, even though he had to treat his pain with morphine. He couldn't bend to put his shoes on but the boys did that for him each morning and off he'd go to work. By September 2004, Dad's doctors decided that he needed a course of radiotherapy for his back, so Tim and Matthew brought him down to Sydney.

'Don't worry, Gem,' they reassured me over the phone the night before they left. 'It's not that serious. It's just a different treatment.'

But I had a very bad feeling. 'I'm going to come out,' I said. 'I'll be on the first plane I can.'

Nothing they could say would dissuade me. Richard was brilliant. I told him that I needed to leave as soon as possible and was going to take the Riverside Bus to Kenya – the slightly faster bus that had replaced the old 'express' to Nairobi.

'Of course you have to go to your father,' he said. 'But you're not catching the bus. I'll take you to the airport.' We settled Nathaniel with Scola – the wonderful girl who lives with us and looks after the children while I work – bundled up Jackob and drove straight to Nairobi, arriving there as night was falling. All night we waited. I was on the waiting list for every flight and every flight remained frustratingly full. I felt powerless and isolated, with no knowledge of what was happening in Sydney. Richard's strong, steady presence kept me going through the night. Babies are great in these sorts of situations too. They don't have any idea what's going on but they still need warmth and food and sleep and, in attending to their little needs and fusses, you can lose yourself for a time.

The next morning, I finally got a seat on a flight that took me first to South Africa and then, after a wait of some hours, to

Sydney. I don't know what I was thinking during that flight. Perhaps Dad was responding well to the new treatment and I'd just have a nice visit with him while he was still himself and return home. But, somewhere in a sad corner of my heart, I knew that we were nearing the end.

I arrived in Sydney and, in a sleep-deprived daze, hailed a taxi and asked to be taken straight to Royal North Shore Hospital. When he saw me preparing to hold Jackob on my lap, the taxi driver was horrified. 'Here, lady, you can't do that. You'll need to order a special taxi with a baby capsule. I could lose my licence.'

I said patiently, 'I've been travelling for over 25 hours from Africa with a baby and am on my way to see my father who has cancer. If we are stopped by the police I will explain this and that it is my fault and not yours. So, can you please just take me to the hospital *RIGHT NOW*?!'

I arrived at the hospital, stashed all my luggage in a toilet – I couldn't think of what else to do with it as the ladies at the administration desk refused to help me – and went off to find Dad. Fortunately, my little brother Danny, who had been by Dad's side since his arrival at the hospital, spotted me. From the way he hugged me I knew it wasn't going to be good news.

'I'm so sorry, Gem, he's already unconscious. But thank God you got here now. Come on, I'll take you up to him.'

No one knew quite what had happened. He had his first radiotherapy treatment after which, while I was on the plane, he inexplicably filled with fluid and slipped into unconsciousness.

I entered his room. Mum was by his side. 'He's very sick, Gem,' she said, raising her face to mine. 'But he has waited for you.'

'Hi Dad,' I said softly, to my unconscious father. 'I'm here.' I gave him a kiss and held little Jackob across the bed to kiss him too. Dad's eyelids fluttered and opened. He didn't speak but he kissed us both and held my eyes with his. A few seconds later they closed again. He died the following morning.

We were all there at the hospital – all my brothers and me. They were all such wonderful men and it made me realise how lucky I was to have them as my siblings. Mum and Dad's immediate family were also around giving all the support and love they could, so it was a wonderful send-off for Dad. We'd all made it to see him. While my heart was aching, I was also thankful that I'd made it in time to say goodbye. I felt quite at peace. We were all grateful as well that the end came so quickly. Dad had been in court only a few days before he died, and then his sudden downturn and death were all over in a short period of time. A man like he was – strong and proud and active – could never have coped with months of being bedridden and dependent.

Dad's funeral – at Armidale cathedral – was an amazing reflection and celebration of his life. It's a huge, imposing cathedral, but on that day it was packed to the rafters and people had to spill outside onto the forecourt. Outside the cathedral, the police formed a guard of honour. We'd had a special coffin made with extra handles and all of Dad's seven boys carried it together into the church with Mum and me behind them. Draped over the coffin was the best ribbon that any of us has won, saying 'State Champion', which had been awarded to my eldest brother, Tim, at a very early age. Alongside it were some other special things my father was associated with, such as some fine merino wool and his favourite rosary beads, symbols of his land and his faith.

There were the lawyers and barristers – his professional colleagues – in their city suits. There were the guys from the side shows – a bit of a rough mob but they just loved him. People from the showjumping years. A bunch of shearers showed up to pay their respects – not only because he'd always been willing to work alongside them but also because he could thrash them at pool.

And a big bunch of Aboriginal fellas – some of them pretty wild, with bad reputations around town – to whom Dad had always given time and helped in whatever way he could, by giving them work or defending them in court. He had affected so many different people in his life, because he was blind to social distinction; to him, there were just people.

I found it hard to imagine a life without Dad. We were similar in some ways – both active and impatient – but he was more forgiving than I am, and more willing to give people his time. Hardly a day goes by when I don't seek his advice, even long after he's gone. If something seems impossible, I think, *What would Dad do in this situation?* and it's often all I need to get me going again. His picture is on the wall in front of my desk next to the picture he gave me of St Jude. The three of us make a great team.

I'm still learning from him.

CHAPTER TEN

After the funeral, I was longing to get back to Tanzania, to be surrounded by my husband and my boys. With one more tie linking me to Australia severed, I felt more than ever that I was returning home. The children, their parents and the staff welcomed me back with gifts of sympathy: piles of home-grown vegetables and eggs, kangas and dresses. These people with so little to give showed me such generosity and kindness. I also discovered that on the day Dad died, the school had cancelled normal lessons out of respect and instead held a special prayer service. It was very moving for me to realise that the school had become such a close and supportive community. It might seem as though we at St Jude's were always in the position of being the givers, but in reality we were given so much back in return.

But I also discovered that while I was away the building work had again gone disastrously wrong. Before I'd left, I'd made sure that Julius – the foreman – would be able to continue drawing down advances in my absence to pay his workmen, the brickies, carpenters and electricians who were fitting out the classrooms.

When I arrived home, I was immediately besieged by angry *fundi*s from all sides.

'Mama, we are hungry.'

'Mama, we have not been paid for two months.'

'Mama, where is our money?'

Also, just before I had left, a team of workers had begun drilling a bore hole for a reliable source of water in the dry season. Water is everything here – as it is in Australia. Not only were we a school but we also were a farm, dependent on our own produce to feed the children and staff. Everything had been proceeding to plan, but I now discovered that as soon as I'd gone the workmen had pulled out the bore drill, without even casing the hole properly first, and disappeared, never to be seen again. The hole had promptly caved in, taking a $US5000 investment with it.

I was devastated. How could these people take advantage of me again? And what a terrible disappointment Julius had been. He'd seemed so trustworthy. But what had clearly happened was that he'd taken $4000 of the school's money, signed for it, and told the workers that while I was away no one was being paid as there was no money in the office.

Of course I sacked him on the spot. And I told the builders that they would have to take it up with him because I couldn't pay twice for the same job. I suspect he got a few bruises and they were able to recoup at least some of the money they were owed.

While I couldn't pay the builders twice, I did offer them ongoing employment, and this time I would pay them directly. I felt ripped off, gullible and very angry that money so generously donated had been wasted. I had some fleeting, satisfying thoughts about revenge. But then I remembered what my dad would say in these circumstances: 'Remember, Gemma, that this too shall pass.' And I let that thought sink in, hotheaded Scorpio though

I am: 'This too shall pass.' The best of times, the worst of times, all would be equally insignificant in the great scheme of things. I felt a weight lift from my shoulders.

From now on I would never forget what Dad taught me about not putting others into a position where they might be tempted into wrongdoing. I would work out how much each column would cost, and pay the brickie myself. I would pay the electrician separately for his work. I would calculate how many bags of cement we would need and physically count off each bag myself. It's really tiring thinking of all the possible things that could go wrong and trying to prevent them, but not nearly as dispiriting as picking up the pieces afterwards.

It was – it is – the most draining aspect of living in Africa, always having to think ahead to foresee how you might possibly be taken advantage of.

For example, one of our drivers, whom I thought was excellent, was taking the children to and from Tengeru, a market-town to the east of Arusha. Unbeknown to me, he would take the children home to Tengeru, then pick up paying passengers for the return journey. This I discovered when he picked up one of Richard's aunts. As he drew into town and asked for her fare she said: 'I'm afraid I can't possibly pay you . . . But do say hello to my nephew Richard.' I would love to have seen his face. Once I heard this, I looked into his records and discovered that, in addition to double-dipping on the fares, he was also siphoning off diesel and selling it.

I could always understand what drove people to do the wrong thing – a predictable mixture of poverty and lack of accountability. Who knows how any of us would behave if we had been brought up in similar circumstances? It made it all the sweeter when people did the right thing and repaid our trust. After the debacle with Julius I kept a number of his team on – his main brickie, Peter, and carpenters Twalib and Festo, who have since become some of the section leaders in my building team. They took over the building work and, knowing that we needed a new classroom block and accommodation for long-term volunteers finished in time for the beginning of the 2005 school year, took it upon themselves to sleep at the school and work in shifts through the night. I didn't realise what they were doing, but when I was told it gave me one of the biggest thrills I'd had in all the time of building the school. I then organised for cooks to come in to prepare their dinner and I tried to make them as comfortable as possible, but that first initiative was theirs alone. They had pride in their work and a sense of responsibility to me and the school. They have gone on to build another block of eight classrooms, two blocks of long-term visitors' rooms, a five-storey water tower, completed a hall with kitchen and store rooms, and a ten-foot-high security wall around the campus. They are a pleasure to work with – easygoing and peaceable but able to adapt to new ideas without a problem.

There was one strange incident around this time. Soon after we bought the block of land for the volunteer houses – from Richard's younger brother Godfrey – Baba came to see me, looking serious.

'What is it, Baba? What can I do for you?' I asked.

He replied slowly: 'I know that you weren't aware of this, Gemma, but just next to where you are planning to build is actually a gravesite. There are two men buried beneath it and it's disrespectful to cover their graves with bricks and cement debris.'

I felt the hairs rising on the back of my neck. Suddenly, my mother's strange words before my wedding came back to me – that the school was built over the graves of two people who hadn't made their peace with God. Was there really something more in it than the last-ditch attempt of a mother trying to prevent her daughter from leaving the country?

'How can I tell where the graves are, Baba? Show me what to do.'

Baba pointed out the special plants that traditionally are planted at the corners of someone's grave. 'See here, here and here. Those are three of the corners of the grave. The fourth plant must have died but it would have been about here,' and he pointed with a stick.

I felt terrible about having unwittingly desecrated the burial site and immediately ordered the builders to remove the rubble from the area and make sure nothing would be placed on it again. Then I went to Richard and asked what he knew about the two men.

'Not a lot,' he said. 'I think they were my great-uncles. I can't remember much about them but I do remember them once locking me and some of the other kids in the house and not feeding us. Mama would know more.'

But when I asked Mama about the men, she started weeping and said they were evil. She would go no further. I didn't want to upset her any more than I had so I left it at that, grateful that my mother's priest had predicted this and that Mum had had the foresight to protect us with those nine masses before the wedding.

I approached the end of 2004 with a sense of cautious optimism. When I'd first started the school, I'd had a plan. Each year we would take on two new Standard 1 classes, so each year we would need to build two new classrooms. Well, in 2004 alone, we had built twelve classrooms, half a hall, connected the school to the Internet and started building housing for the staff and visitors.

We'd also introduced hot lunches. We'd noticed that some children were not concentrating as well as they might have been and that others were afflicted with the kinds of skin complaints associated with lack of proper nutrition. After we made the expensive decision to feed every child and staff member a good hot lunch every day – usually a stew of some sort with rice or *ugali* – the children's health and concentration increased dramatically. For the first time ever, I had a wonderful building team in place whom I could trust and who had repaid that trust. Between September and December, we'd selected another 150 new students who would start in the new year, taking our numbers up to about 500. We'd had more than our share of glitches on the way but things seemed to be running smoothly now. I could breathe a sigh of relief.

Another cause for celebration was more personal: my triumph in getting a special little girl called Jesca to stay on at the school. Jesca came to the school in 2004. She'd been top of the class at her government school up on Mount Meru and was not just intelligent but had the sort of attitude that you needed to get ahead as a poor young girl in Africa. Jesca brought with her two other girls from her class: Irene, who'd been ranked number two, and Mercy, who'd been number three even though she'd been badly disabled by polio and had missed a lot of schooling.

Because both of her parents had died, Jesca lived with two of her uncles and her Maasai grandmother, up on the mountain. In addition to her schoolwork, Jess had to keep house for the two men and the elderly woman. She coped amazingly well and was a child we had great hopes for until one day the uncles decided that educating a girl was useless. They pulled her out of school so she could keep house for them full-time. Jess was nine years old.

I've never been especially soft and fuzzy or lovey-dovey with the children. I've always made sure I had other people around me who are better at that side of things. I'm more likely to have a joke with the kids than to sit down and cuddle them, but when they're in trouble I will fight for them till the bitter end.

I've had a few of these situations over the years, especially with Maasai fathers who often don't believe in education for their girls, but in this case, with such a gifted child, it bordered on criminal waste. I drove straight to the uncles' house, up winding paths through banana palms, and confronted them.

'What do you think you're doing taking Jesca out of school?' I demanded.

'Who else will wash our clothes?' one of the uncles replied, unmoved.

'I don't actually care about your clothes,' I said. 'I care about this child, this extremely able, intelligent child, going to waste as an unpaid servant. Just think how short-sighted you're being. Use your heads. This girl is going to do something really special with her life. When you're old, she's the one who is going to be taking care of the whole family. If you don't do it for her, do it for yourselves – it's an investment for you to make sure she has a good education.'

'Say what you like. We're the ones who are in charge, and we say she's finished with school,' said the other uncle.

I felt frustrated and close to tears but couldn't get any further with such pig-headed obstinacy, so I called on the *mwenyekiti wa kijiji*, or village chairman, to adjudicate. The chairman is like my father-in-law here in Moshono. He's the one you go to for all official transactions or proceedings – if you're buying land, for example, or if a thief has been caught or a marriage broken down. The chairman of this area gave the matter some thought and then made his pronouncement.

'The girl must return to school. Her uncles are not to hinder her education or to retaliate in any way and they must not come near the school.' He turned to me, 'Don't worry. She'll be back at school tomorrow.'

I didn't quite believe the chairman. It was one thing for him to tell these stubborn and ignorant chauvinists what to do and quite another to expect them to comply.

The next morning, I waited for the buses to come in. 'Mrs Richard!' I heard a happy voice yell. It was Jesca, leaping down from the bus and racing over to give me a big hug. It was a great result. I know you're not supposed to have favourites, but after you've fought for someone you can't help but feel an extra bond with them, and I'll always care about Jess and her future now.

So that was a triumph for education over ignorance. Now all I needed was to sort out my staffing problems and I'd be set for 2005. Kim had gone home earlier in the year – unable to subsist any longer on no pay and credit card extensions – and had left behind her a huge gap. By the end of 2004, Ange too had to go back to Australia, to clear her debts and to study. Ange had been our headmistress for three years since she'd arrived for the opening of the school in early 2002 and had been so fantastic with students and their parents – tough but fair – that it was incredible to think she was only 21.

I would have loved them both to have stayed – for my own selfish reasons – but in a way I was glad that they were going. I knew that while they were here, the rest of their lives was on hold. For me, Africa is my home. I am married to an African man, my children are Tanzanian. I don't have a 'real life' to resume at some later date or a hole to explain on my CV. This is my life.

It's always been hard here, getting the right sort of volunteers. People like Kim, Ange, Edwina, Charlotte, our bursar who came over in May 2004 for four months and is still here eighteen months later, and Karin, our Sponsorship Coordinator who came out for a few months and is also still here, are very special people. They need to be calm and balanced, flexible and utterly without expectations of what might happen next. Most of the time they are doing things that are not a part of their job description and this is what makes them so valuable. People who live their lives by a rigid schedule or people who are thrown when the unexpected happens can't cope at all in Africa. Then there are the other factors you can't anticipate, like the effects of the climate on people, or a particularly nasty bout of illness. Those best suited to this life can take it all in their stride, while the others fall by the wayside.

After we'd built a house for the volunteers to live in – with a shower and toilet, both of which sometimes even worked – and our volunteer program became more widely known, we also had an influx of kids who saw a stint in Africa as something like a Kontiki Tour: an excuse for a lot of cheap beer and photo opportunities with some cute kids. They're the ones who complain when the hot water runs out and leave the volunteer house in a mess, expecting staff to clean up behind them. When I think of how uncomplaining the early volunteers were, sleeping in tents, washing in buckets and cooking over a fire, I can get a bit impatient with these pampered backpackers but the situation is entirely predictable and of my own making.

Some people come out to Africa with the best of intentions but for the wrong reasons. You don't discover until it's too late that they are escaping from something – a bad marriage, some personal or professional baggage or crisis – and they expect Africa to heal their wounds or at least provide a refuge. There are a lot of sad, damaged expats living here, as well as some who are truly inspiring.

Filling Ange's shoes was always going to be difficult. None of our existing local teachers was ready to step up into the principal's role, so we needed to find someone from outside. The hard thing about employing someone from overseas is that a candidate can look great on a CV, or interview well, but how can you foresee whether they'll be able to handle life in Africa?

We had a number of good applications but an outstanding one from a headmaster in Wales, whose name was David. He had three degrees and was tremendously enthusiastic about what we were doing and what he could bring to the school. We hadn't seen him in action but we were desperate. When could he start?

Ange stayed on until early in the new year to hand over the reins to David. He seemed perfectly nice, though not quite what we'd expected. He was perhaps a little fussier than we'd hoped, and a bit more vulnerable-seeming. He didn't really appear to be a man who was going to take charge, but we had to give him the benefit of the doubt. Then we sent Ange off with a grand farewell, attended by all the students and their family members. Initially, I'd sent out an open invitation but when we received more than 3000 replies, I limited numbers to one family member per child. It was the most beautiful commemoration to a wonderful teacher. Every family had brought her a gift – chickens, vegetables and fabric – and the queue of people waiting to give her their present snaked out the school gate and around the corner.

I had about six weeks at the school with David before I had to go back to Australia for the annual Rotary conferences. There was no way I could miss them. We were – again, when weren't we? – just scraping by financially. Our building program was still expanding rapidly and I'd had to buy most of our materials on credit, cashing in on some of the goodwill I'd built up over the last few years. We'd received one amazing donation over Christmas from a priest in Sydney, Father Tony Doherty, who'd raised $10,000 in his parish, and one of the things I wanted to do back in Australia was to show him where the money had gone: into six new classrooms that formed the top part of a twelve-classroom block.

So I crossed my fingers, left the inexperienced new head-master in charge of the school and flew to Sydney. When I arrived, I contacted Father Tony and offered to come to all of his masses that Sunday to show his congregation a PowerPoint presentation of the school and the classrooms their money had helped to build. Then I set off to Moss Vale to give a talk at a Rotary conference. It was a Saturday. After the conference, there was a dinner, and another talk. I didn't make it to bed until 2 am, in the uneasy knowledge that I had to be at a 7 am mass in Sydney.

'Don't do it,' Ange had said that evening on the phone from Coogee where she was back living with her parents. 'No one goes to early mass anyway except for a couple of old grandmothers.'

'Nah, I've got to,' I said. 'I owe it to Father Tony and I'd really like to meet him.'

So Ange arranged to meet me in the morning in Sydney to drive me to church. I set my alarm for 3.30 am.

I have to say that, looking around the church – St Mary Magdalene's in Rose Bay – Ange was right. There were only about six people but it was still lovely. And after mass, one young bloke – *not* a grandmother – came up to talk.

'I think that what you're doing out there sounds really good,' he said. 'Can I give you a donation?'

'Yeah, no worries,' I said. 'That would be great.'

'I'll just nip home and get my chequebook, then, and catch you at the next mass,' he said.

I didn't think any more about it until Ange and I were setting up the projector for the next PowerPoint viewing.

'Umm, can I make my donation now?' It was the young bloke from before. He was probably only 30 or so.

'Sure,' I said. 'Make it out to Rotary if you want it to be tax deductible.'

It took a few seconds for the fog to clear in front of my eyes enough to see what he'd written: *twenty thousand dollars*! It was the biggest single donation we'd ever received. We were in the front pew of a church and people were pouring in for ten o'clock mass and there was me, going berserk, jumping all over this young man, who I found out later was called Craig Chapman.

'We need to buy a bus. Can we buy a bus? What's your favourite colour?'

'Do what you like with it. It's your money. And red,' he said.

It was great. I sent the money straight over to Charlotte, our school bursar, and she told Richard to start looking for the bus which would become the big red bus. I wouldn't classify that one as a St Jude's moment exactly but I do thank God I went to the early mass on one-and-a-half hours' sleep. It showed me that it is worth pulling your finger out and doing everything to the utmost. You can never slacken off because you never know where a fantastic opportunity might be hiding.

While I was away, I tried not to worry too much about the school and David. However competent he might have been back in Wales, I was aware that this was a very different experience for him. He knew nothing of the culture of the country or the no-less-powerful culture of the school. I tried to have faith that everything would be all right but was apprehensive about what I might find on my return home. At least we had so many safe-guards and systems in place by this stage, I told myself, that the school could almost run itself.

Well, no, it couldn't. Not without someone cracking the occasional whip. In two short months, St Jude's had become a shambles. The chaos I discovered on my return made earlier disasters pale into insignificance. At least they had only been disasters relating to building work. This was a mess that threatened the running of the school itself and put in jeopardy its continued existence.

Teachers weren't turning up for classes on time. Committee reports were not getting written. The toilets weren't being cleaned. The quality of the food had dropped dramatically. Children were turning up for school in different-coloured pants and shoes. There were piles of notes on my desk from parents complaining that their children were not getting any homework.

I discovered that some of the teachers had gone to David demanding pay rises, which he had simply given them. A new teacher – Phillip – had started at the school and, instead of putting him on probation, David had immediately put him on contract. Of course Phillip abused what had been given to him so easily and didn't turn up to some of his classes. On my return David even came up to me and said that Phillip should have a pay rise, as 'all the other teachers have been given one'. I had only ever given increased pay in response to improved work ethic or increased work load and certainly not in response to pressure.

Normally, we have a system where, in addition to their other duties, each teacher is in charge of one non-academic aspect of the school's running. So you might be an English teacher but you also have responsibility for making sure the toilets are cleaned properly, or you could be a maths teacher but you have to check that children are wearing the correct uniform. Teachers file a report on their area every month. It's a good way of keeping an eye on all the little details that can otherwise be overlooked, and making everyone accountable. It's also a great way for me to receive constructive feedback because I can't be everywhere at once.

David didn't like the system. I think he felt that we needed to do more trusting and less overseeing, so he removed all our checking and reporting procedures and relied on goodwill to keep things running smoothly. I tried to make him see that his way wasn't working. It's doubtful whether it would work in any country, let alone Tanzania, as every good business has to have quality assurance procedures. His goodwill was being abused. Even though the teachers liked him – well, they would, wouldn't they? They'd had pay increases and were only doing half their jobs – they didn't respect him.

Also David didn't believe in the importance of homework. In Western countries, dealing with primary school children, he'd be in line with a lot of people's views. But this is Africa. The parents strongly believe in homework. Who are we to come to their country and tell them that their way is wrong?

The situation reached crisis point in the middle of the night, only a few days after I'd returned from Australia. I was woken by a phone call saying that there were some parents in the village pub – representatives of the Parents' Committee – who wanted to speak to me. I set off to the pub to hear what they had to say.

They'd heard, their spokesman said, that there were five teachers in the school who were going to demand another pay rise from David and, if they didn't receive it, they were going to leave.

I wasn't sure what reassurance the parents wanted from me but I had to speak truthfully. 'That's fine. They're not going to get a pay rise and if they want to leave, then I'm not going to stop them.'

'That's what we wanted to say to you, Mrs Richard,' said another parent. 'If any of these troublesome teachers want to leave, you just let them go. We will come in and help you teach the classes. Don't think that you have to go and find new teachers quickly. We will be there for two, three, four months, for as long as it takes for you to find the quality of teachers that you want. The parents are behind you 100 percent.'

I was really moved. When I'd first started St Jude's, one of my main aims was to encourage parents to feel involved in the school. I had wanted them to be able to bring up concerns and questions without the fear that their child would suffer any ill consequences. One of the ways we'd addressed this was with the Parents' Committee, where issues could be raised anonymously.

With most of the parents illiterate and traditionally uncomfortable in a school environment, I'd never been quite sure how successful I'd been in fostering a sense of community ownership of the school, but here was the proof. These parents, unschooled as they were, were prepared to take the place of teachers and help keep discipline in the school. For the first time, I realised what a strong force they were, how much they cared about the school, and how lucky I was to have them on my side.

Also, while some of the local teachers had let me down and allowed their standards to slip as soon as they saw they could get away with it, many others had risen to the challenge. It was interesting to see which ones were strong and which were merely followers. A few teachers who had always kept their heads down and avoided attention were the ones who had the courage to go against their fellow teachers and come to me and say: 'I'm concerned about the way discipline is slipping,' or 'I've only been here for three months, but I've already seen a big decrease in uniform standards.'

One of the teachers who caught my eye was a new teacher called Nestory Msoffe. He'd only joined us at the end of 2004, as a Kiswahili teacher, and had already impressed me with his quiet dignity and air of maturity. During this period, he had the courage to stand up against his peers for the benefit of the school as a whole. He was clearly a leader and not a follower.

We called a staff meeting, and brought in some of the members of our school board, all Tanzanian. First there was Bibi Hans, who is the chairman of the board (I am the director of the school but just a member of the board). Bibi is a wonderful and strong woman. She is a scientist, her husband is a doctor and they've funded Maasai medical clinics in the area. At one of those clinics, they found Emiliana, a young girl who was being abused. Bibi Hans came to me and said that she would house her if I could educate her, which we've done. She's a great little girl, number one or two constantly in her class. Then there was the head of the Parents' Committee, Bibi Anna, a representative from the Ministry of Education, Mr Saumu, and a district school inspector, Mr Minja. Mr Minja is from Moshono and, even though he's become a big man in the wider district, he still has a soft spot for us and puts the pressure on me by inspecting our work, which I love. We all need to be kept up to the mark by someone.

Bibi Hans called the staff to order and said to them: 'I understand there are teachers among you who are dissatisfied with your conditions. We wish to say to you, if you want to leave, then go. You will be paid to the end of the month. We are not going to handcuff you to your desks. However, we will not give in to pressure for pay rises. Pay rises will only be given as a reward for good work for those who deserve it – and at the appropriate time.'

The teachers looked at the ground. There was some shuffling of feet. But they made no response, then or ever, as they are paid very well. Not one teacher left . . . except for David.

I blamed myself entirely for the problems we had. I made the mistake of putting someone who had never set foot in Africa before in a management position where people were able to take advantage of him. When anyone arrives in Africa, they have to go through a seasoning process. They have to be 'burned', to be ripped off and ripped off again before they start to understand the culture here. David had too much responsibility too soon and the problems that arose were entirely preventable.

When David went, at Easter, we were left with a legacy of bad habits. Some of the teachers in the school had only known it under his leadership so they needed to be educated into new systems, others needed to be reminded of the way things had run before. I didn't replace him with a new head teacher. Instead, I eventually elevated Nestory Msoffe to Academic Master – as he, like some other teachers, had proved himself to me to be a true leader. He was to work with the already elevated school deputy, Ben Mainga, who deals with the non-academic issues of the school such as cleaning, welfare, grounds, food quality and discipline. Gradually, I have given them more and more responsibilities so that now I only really have to solve serious issues and help run the Wednesday staff meetings. Eventually, if I did invite one of them to be headmaster, we'd both know that he was well-trained, confident and able to do the job.

Nestory, in particular, flourished in his new position as Academic Master of the school. In addition to his clearcut academic responsibility for over 50 staff, coordinating meetings with heads of departments and so on, one of his most important roles became that of diplomacy – smoothing the sometimes jagged edges where teaching staff and administration met, and bridging the cultural gap between Western and African teachers. There have been so many times when his help has been invaluable. He has a great rapport with the District and Regional Education officers and his experience with Tanzanian examinations is a real resource for us.

Within the staff, Nestory coordinates many different personalities, people from different nationalities and religions and tribal backgrounds – only someone with his palpable air of fairness and calmness could do it. It makes him ideally suited to being part of our staff support and discipline team. We set this team up, post-David, to deal immediately with staff personality problems – a clash between a Maasai and a Chagga staff member, for example – or issues like punctuality or lesson preparation, before they had a chance to become entrenched. It worked wonderfully well and, with the reintroduction of our other systems, as well as new programs initiated by Nestory, it wasn't long before St Jude's was back on track. The staff support and discipline team has grown to five and really helps solve problems in the school before they get a chance to worsen. They work confidently and without my presence. Clearly it is hard for the teachers to discipline their peers but it is also a great platform for us to see who is leadership material, so that we can train more future leaders of the school, in keeping with our mission of teaching local people how to run good schools.

CHAPTER ELEVEN

For me, 2005 was a roller-coaster of a year. It was the year in which we had been threatened with a mass staff walk-out, and the year we finished building our school hall. It was the year in which we received our biggest-ever donation, enabling us to start planning ahead for a completely new second campus so that we can help another 1000-plus kids in the future, and the year my beloved first group of children 'graduated' from Standard 4 and we were able to glimpse what they might be able to achieve. It was also the year when I came as close as I've ever come to throwing the whole thing in.

I actually think I would give it all up – the school, the children, love them though I do – if I thought my work damaged my relationship with my husband or my own children. It's something I've had to examine over and over. I'm not unaware of the irony of handing my children over to their nanny, Scola, so I can go and put in a twelve-hour day on behalf of other people's children. And yet – Scola needs the work. She sends the money home to support a whole family. My children could not be happier, if you judge by their rambunctious behaviour and tireless appetite for life. I have built the school around myself and my home so that, like it or not, I'm at its very core. I can delegate aspects of the school's running but I can't expect anyone else to feel as I do about it.

I'm very lucky because Richard allows me a lot of freedom. It can't be easy to be married to someone who has such an all-consuming passion outside the marriage. But he's never been anything but supportive of my other life, despite his natural inclinations, which are quite possessive. On a few occasions when we were first going out, I saw that side of him. One evening in Uganda, Richard, Gertrude and I had been leaving a nightclub when a man gave me a casual flick on the bum. I turned around to say something but Richard already had him on the floor. Another time, he dealt very quickly and violently with a drunken soldier who'd been shouting abuse at me. Before we met, Richard had a reputation as a hard man, the sort it wouldn't be wise to cross. Knowing this side of Richard's character, I realise what an effort it must have been for him to allow me the freedom he does, and I appreciate it even more.

Married women in Tanzania are more accountable for their actions to their husbands than in the West. Early on in our married life, I'd be off somewhere, tracking down a government official for a paper or inspecting bricks, and I wouldn't have told Richard where I was. When I returned that evening, he'd say, not angrily but with a bit of puzzlement: 'Gemma, I had no idea where you were today.'

I'd say, 'Gosh, I'm sorry Rich, it just happened and I didn't think of calling in.' But it made me think about his feelings and how it might be unsettling to have a wife who is off all day engaged in unknown business. So now I try to let Richard know what I'll be doing – as far as possible – and give him an account of my day in the evening. I don't mind letting him know my movements. His concern is just a reflection of his protective nature. I'm aware that if I was African I wouldn't be able to do half of what I do. I couldn't drive around the country the way I do, or have the sort of business relationships with men I have. If, in return, I have to have a cosy chat with my husband in the evening to keep him in the loop, it's hardly a big price to pay.

I had a glimpse of what life might have been like if I'd been a real Tanzanian wife when one of the St Jude's teachers, Lucy, was getting married. A few of us from school went to her hen's party, which was a new experience for me and the other Westerners at the school. One of the best things about the party was the advice for new brides she received – all of it traditional Tanzanian wisdom which bore a distinct resemblance to *The Australian Women's Weekly* circa 1928.

One of Lucy's friends – an older and wiser married woman – handed out slips of paper with gems like: 'If your husband has been out with his friends and comes home at 3 am, don't reproach him. Instead, make sure you are beautifully dressed and have prepared a good dinner. Tell him how sorry you are that he had to stay out late and bring him his slippers.' We Westerners were saying, 'Then go and get a cricket bat!' but the Tanzanians took it all seriously.

Another piece of advice was: 'Ask your husband what his favourite food is and take care and love while preparing it because the love will flow through him and back to you. For this reason, *don't* allow the maid to cook for him!'

It was clear that a typical Tanzanian marriage was not supposed to be a partnership, in our understanding of the word. The woman had to be totally accommodating. She was supposed to remove her husband's shoes when he came in the door and wash him when he bathed. I'm more likely to say, 'You're a big boy, Rich. You know how to wash yourself, don't you?' And if

I know Richard's out drinking with his mates, I'm not going to make a fuss. The most I'll do is to put his dinner in a thermos and go to bed.

But at the same time, I do make a big effort to give Richard love and time, because I'm aware I'm home a lot less than most African wives. I'll often say to the girls in the office, 'I'm just popping home for ten minutes to give Richard a bit of love,' and I try to keep Sundays free so that we can do things as a family. I've no idea why our partnership works so well – we're both extremely hot-headed, determined, independent people, so the relationship could have ended in fireworks – but we just mesh beautifully together.

I'm slightly uncomfortable when people assume that being married to an African man is somehow different or exotic. I'm not living out of the film *The White Masai*. Whatever our backgrounds, Rich and I are just two people working at our marriage like anybody else. We're a team – although sometimes I'll let him think he's the ultimate decision-maker. There is no way I could do what I do without him. I have never had to coax him along, he's just always been totally supportive of what I've done. Having an African side and a Western side to our partnership has given us a great advantage in so many aspects of our life over here. Things I can't do as a Westerner, Rich can do. Things he can't do as a Tanzanian, I've got covered.

For example, if we need to buy a bus, Richard will do the haggling. If I try to buy it, the vendors will charge me three times the price. But then I'll get the paperwork for the bus through whichever government department controls those transactions, because Africans don't mind keeping another African waiting – all day if they feel like it – but they won't make a Westerner sit for hours on a splintery bench. Sometimes I'll get a bit big-headed and think: *I can do the haggling on my own, I've been here for long enough now*, but I'd be fooling myself. I'm okay doing a bit of bargaining at the vegetable markets, but as far as big purchases go? Forget it. It's the way it will always be.

When our second container-load of goods came over from Australia, I knew we'd be better off sending Richard to clear the container through Customs than for me to do it myself. It's a hideous job. I said to him (I was pregnant with Jackob at the time): 'Rich, what's the worst thing that I'm going to ask you to do as my husband?'

He looked panic-stricken. 'Help deliver the baby?'

'No, Richard. Just go down to Dar es Salaam to clear the container.'

If a Westerner tried to do it, they'd be whacked with taxes and import charges, the paperwork would be 'lost' and the officials would need a $2000 inducement to 'find' it again. Richard, being an African, isn't presumed to have any money. Also, he always seems to know a handy old school friend in the right place.

Similarly, last Christmas, Ange suggested to the sponsors that they buy a goat for their sponsored student as a gift. Nice idea, Ange, because a roasted goat for Christmas would be a very exciting thing, but I've told her that next time she can come over and buy all the beasts!

Richard and I went to the markets and he said, 'All right, Gem. You buy two goats and I'll buy eight. I bet you $10 that you won't be able to buy one of your goats cheaper than any of my eight.'

'Done,' I said, my competitive blood up.

We headed off in different directions into the markets. All the Maasai had come down from the mountain, each of them with just one or two goats for sale. I pulled out my best negotiating skills and finally managed to get one goat for $18 and one for $16, which I thought was a great bargain.

What was interesting was that there was a price at which the goat-traders were prepared to sell to me but they would not accept anything lower, even if it meant they didn't sell their one animal that day. I said to one man: 'I'll give you $16 for that animal.'

'No. The price is $20,' he replied.

'$16 or nothing,' I said, and walked away. Far from following me, when I looked back, he was happily negotiating with Richard to sell the same goat for $13! The most Richard paid for any of them was $13, and the least was $11.

I just don't understand that mentality. Africans are prepared to shoot themselves in the foot for the sake of their perception that because Westerners have more they should pay more.

So on that occasion, Richard won the bet and I have to accept that there are some things he'll always be able to do better than me. He's very welcome to buy the goats.

I still get very excited when I see Richard, probably because we have longer times apart than many couples. As part of his safari work, he's had to handle a big range of different personality types, which has made him very easygoing. He's also both more cynical and more forgiving than I am, qualities he's tried to pass on to me. If you expect the worst and realise that you're going to be ripped off then, when it happens, it's much easier to accept and move on. If you go on naively believing the best of people and then your trust is betrayed, it's easy to become embittered in this country. Once that happens, you're not much good for anyone, least of all yourself.

When I first married Richard, a man I knew came up to me and said: 'My wife has died and I'm desperate for money for her funeral. I really need $10.'

I'd seen him sitting in the pew in front of me at church, which was a pretty rock-solid recommendation in my book, so I thought, *Why not?*

I gave him the money but soon found out that his wife was hale and hearty and he'd just scammed me out of $10. The next time

I saw him at church, I wondered whether he'd be ashamed or defiant, but he was completely brazen and greeted me cheerfully, as if nothing had ever happened. It happens time and time again and I'm only now starting to be able to accept it.

It's not that I don't understand the reasons for it. People here have so little and their lives are so hard. And then they see the wealthy Westerners, here for a luxury safari, who hand out $20 to children on the street because they're made uncomfortable by their poverty, not realising that they're contributing to a corrupt, hand-out mentality. All Westerners are seen as rich pickings. Most Africans' images of our lives are largely drawn from glimpses of shop-front televisions, showing the worst excesses of *Dallas*-style soap operas. I've tried to make people believe that we don't all live like that – that some of us actually cook for ourselves and clean our own houses – but I'm greeted with disbelief.

I once said to Richard, 'Rich, I've only been here for five years and already I'm exhausted and burnt out and feel like I've been cheated a million times. How am I going to be able to cope with another 40 years of it?'

He replied, calmly as always, 'By not expecting things to change all at once. Maybe eventually they will but not in our life-times. Even if you're here for 70 years, there will always be people wanting to take advantage of you just because you're white. There's no point dwelling on it. It's just the way it is. It will drive you to illness if you take it personally or you try to change the mentality quickly.'

Richard never keeps things bottled up inside. If I've done something he doesn't like, he tells me straight away and then never thinks about it again. He's helped me to understand Africa but never gives me rules about the way things are done here or makes me feel like I've transgressed any cultural taboos with my behaviour. I've been incredibly lucky.

But on Richard's side, he also appreciates the freedom that comes from being married to a non-Tanzanian woman. Because I trust Richard completely, I've never minded him having his boys' time. I have seven brothers and I totally understand the need for men to have time on their own. I know he needs to go off with his mates and drink beer and smoke cigarettes (which he'd deny, even with smoke trailing up from a cigarette hidden behind his back).

Richard tells me that if he were married to a Tanzanian woman, 'she'd be at me all the time to change and telling me that everything I did was wrong. And she'd always be saying, "I need a new dress, I want some gold jewellery". Whereas you, I have to force to buy anything new.' So there's a bit of mutual benefit on both sides.

My boys too are able to pick what they like from African and Australian cultures. It shows in their language, a gorgeous mixture of Swahili and English, or 'Swinglish'. They've probably been out on safari to the national parks 20 times and have seen every African animal there is. Jackob even had his dummy stolen by a baboon. They have no understanding that they're quite privileged to see all this wildlife. They don't consider a lion to be any more exciting than a cow. But actually, their favourite animal is a horse – a genetic throwback to my childhood, maybe, or just the allure of what to them seems exotic.

Nathaniel seems to have inherited his father's amazing ability for spotting wildlife. Richard has incredible peripheral vision. We'll be driving along and suddenly he'll jam on the brakes.

'What it is it, Rich?' I'll say, seeing nothing but waving grass and a few distant trees.

'There, in the fork of that tree 100 metres away. It's a leopard.'

It's the same with our keen-eyed four-year-old. Not long ago, I was driving the children and a few of the volunteers from school in one of the local national parks, all of our eyes peeled to spot animals, when Nathaniel cried out: 'Mummy, Mummy, I can see a dead wildebeest and there's a lion eating it.'

'Did you see anything?' I asked the others. Noooo, they said. Nor had I.

'That's not like you to tell stories, Nathan,' I said.

'I'm not, I'm not,' said Nathaniel, getting a bit teary. 'Turn around and I'll show you.'

'Okay,' I said. 'But if there's no wildebeest, you have to say sorry to Mummy.'

Of course, when we drove back to where he'd first cried out, there *was* a wildebeest, and a lion gnawing on its fresh carcass. I couldn't believe it. None of us had – or would have – spotted it. It must be something in his blood.

But there are some odd parts to bringing up children in Africa. I find it hard to accept a lot of the old wives' tales, which are treated as gospel, when sometimes they seem to make no sense. Babies and young children here are rugged up within an inch of their lives, even on the hottest of days, with beanies and fleeces. If you're ever caught trying to give one of them a cold drink, you're treated as though you were intentionally poisoning them. My mother- and sisters-in-law are always trying to put more layers of clothing on the boys.

On the Western side, I've passed on to the children my love for books and reading, which you wouldn't find in a typical Tanzanian house. But on Richard's side, his grandmother, a little white-haired Maasai lady, sings the children Maasai songs and tells them fables such as how the elephant got his trunk.

They both love mashed potato – my ultimate comfort food – but they also enjoy *ugali* (a traditional flour-based food eaten with your hands). And they love using their fingers with it. They are mad about *makande*, a local dish of mixed corn kernels and kidney beans, but they also love roast dinners and gravy.

I don't know where they'll end up but it seems to me to be a pretty good beginning. I do feel stretched, like any working mother. Scola has been incredible and doesn't let anyone past our house gates; otherwise I'd have builders coming in the door when I've gone to bed. The time I have with Richard and the children in the morning is so special that I don't want anything to disturb it.

The children wake at about 5 am and come and jump into bed with us. I know I should stop it really, but I love it, and so does Richard. The mornings are when we read books and play but it's also when I do my talking with Richard, along the lines of: 'Hi. My name is Gemma. What's yours again?' And vice versa.

Mostly, the balance between the school and my family life seems to work. There's only been one time when I have ever seriously considered the idea that the whole St Jude's project might be a mistake, and that maybe I didn't have the stamina to see it through. It was when I arrived back from Australia to find the mess that David had created as headmaster. While some positives came out of the situation – I discovered the support I had from some of the parents and staff – other parents were angry, many of the teachers were certainly angry and I had to do a great deal of work to undo all the damage.

Underlying it all, what really depressed me was how quickly everything we'd achieved could be destroyed. I had visions of starting similar schools across Tanzania, but if each school was so fragile, so dependent on the right personnel, then how could we possibly get anywhere?

Once you let one doubt creep in, more follow through the crack it has left in your defences. What was the point of it all? We were helping 500, 600, 700 children at St Jude's, but what about the thousands we couldn't reach? Even the ones we did educate, were they going to be able to change the culture in Africa or would they discover it was too hard to swim against the tide and become part of the same corrupt system? What about the children beyond Tanzania, in Uganda and the rest of Africa? The problems facing this continent are so entrenched, how can one school make the least bit of difference?

I actually said to Richard that I was sick of fixing other people's mistakes and could leave St Jude's and go to work for one of the international schools on the other side of Arusha. At the time I was being paid $300 a month and knew that if I went to ISM (the International School of Moshi) or Braeburn, the two main international schools in town, which cater for the UN and expat community, I could be paid nearly ten times that. I could work 9 to 5, five days a week, and even get to spend time with my children and husband.

'You can't leave this, Gemma,' said Richard, and he was only echoing what I already knew in my heart. 'This is your project, this is your purpose on earth. No one will love this school as you do and even though people are going to come and go and there will always be problems, you have to work through it. If you leave, what would happen to the kids?'

He was right, I knew. My life was St Jude's and I could no more leave it than turn away from my own children. But my unfamiliar mood of depression wasn't so easy to shake.

Fortunately, at about this time I had a visit from a good friend, my old English teacher from Inverell, Rosemary Breen.

The Breens – Rosemary and her husband, Laurie, who had been my headmaster – had been great supporters of St Jude's. They were a wonderful couple, originally from England, very devout Catholics and tremendously active socially. They helped prisoners, immigrants, the local Aboriginal community. Wherever there was a need, they came up with a response. The Breens were also very outgoing, outdoorsy people, though to look at Laurie you'd think he was a university professor who spent his days in a library. Rosemary was the one who'd interested me in the Duke of Edinburgh scheme when I was at school, which was probably my start in charity work.

Since the school had begun, the Breens had donated something like $20,000, which was fantastically generous, considering they were retired teachers with a lot of other demands on their resources. On one visit to the school, Rosemary asked what project they could help with.

One of the things at the top of our wish list at that time was a hall. We needed somewhere not just for school assemblies and concerts but also for the children to eat lunch, and that could eventually accommodate a kitchen. At the time, lunch was still cooked in huge pots over open fires in a makeshift outdoor 'kitchen'. I remember pacing out the dimensions of a hall with Rosemary and this is one of the reasons I love Africa. Rather than calling in a team of experts – architects or draughtsmen – Rosemary and I walked the length of a field with a tape measure, saying: 'Well, it might need to seat 500 children one day so let's make it 45 metres long. Wait, if we make it 47, we could fit in another row of children and still leave room for them to go around the back. Let's call it 47 and, whaddya reckon? Sixteen metres wide?' It was an ad hoc method, but it suited me perfectly.

So the Breens donated some money for the hall and it was built in bits and pieces. Then Laurie died, suddenly, on the plane back from a trip to England. It was a tremendous shock. Rosemary asked whether she could fund the rest of the hall and dedicate it to her husband's memory, something I was thrilled to do.

When it was finished, Rosemary returned to see what we'd achieved. It had cost more money than expected, as we'd added a big kitchen at the back of the room, but it was worth it.

We walked together to the hall. It was a fine building, with a soaring tin roof and open sides. Seeing the children lined up there for assemblies never failed to fill me with pride. Rosemary was a great one for hands-on activities and was obviously pleased to see what their donation had created. So was I, but I was still in that phase of self-doubt and worry. I was missing out on vital parts of my own children's childhoods, and for what?

'You know, Rosemary,' I said. 'I look at this hall. It can fit, what, 700 kids? But this project is such a small drop. It's not even a drop. It's not even a grain of sand. It's the smallest thing in the biggest area you can imagine. When I travel away from Arusha, if I'm looking around myself at an airport in Kenya or Australia, I realise that our little school is so tiny, and what it can achieve is so limited, that it's almost a joke.'

Rosemary listened to me thoughtfully. 'Gemma,' she said, and I was reminded of the English teacher she'd been. 'Have you ever heard the story of the starfish?'

'No, I haven't,' I said. 'Is it any good?'

'Two men were once walking along a beach together,' she said in answer. 'It was just after a storm and the beach was strewn with flotsam and jetsam. Stranded all the way along the beach were thousands and thousands of starfish, still alive but slowly drying out in the sun's heat. One of the men walked over them but the other stopped every few paces, picked up a starfish and threw it back into the sea.

' "What are you doing that for?" asked the first man. "You know it's not going to make a difference. There are too many starfish and only one of you."

' "No," agreed his friend, bending down and picking up a starfish. As he placed it in the shallows and picked up another, he said: "But it makes a difference to this one. And this one. And this one." '

I felt hairs prickle on the back of my neck. She was absolutely right. There was no point in looking at the big picture – in Africa, that's the way to go crazy – but if I concentrated on the little picture, on improving the lives of a handful of children, of even one child, then I was doing my job.

At the end of 2005, our first group of children was going to sit their national Standard 4 examination. While that was only a handful of children, hopefully it would be the start of hundreds of children going through Standard 4. Already their chances of a better future were much greater than they'd have been without us. Rather than beating myself up for what I was unable to do, it was much more positive to focus on what we were able to achieve. We might only be able to save a few starfish, but for those individual starfish it means the world, as it's the only chance they've got. If Athumani realises his dream of becoming a pilot or Alex Elifas can make life a little better for his family, then every hour, every dollar spent has been worth it.

'Wow,' I said. 'Thanks, Rosemary.'

CHAPTER TWELVE

Of course, Rosemary's starfish story wasn't a magical spell, casting out every concern I had for St Jude's, but I felt much lighter in spirit and more focussed after I had spoken with my old mentor. All my old enthusiasm came flooding back. Having been bogged down for a time, thinking only about my current troubles and the immediate needs of the school, I was able to take a step back and start thinking about the future again.

It was in this frame of mind that I agreed to appear on the current affairs program, *Australian Story*, when the ABC approached me. In truth, I'm prepared to do anything that will publicise the school and increase the number of people who are helping us educate the children at St Jude's. Every time I've spoken at a function or on a radio program, there's always at least a few new people who approach me afterwards to say they would like to sponsor a child or a teacher. And every single new sponsor is a lifeline to a child.

I think the attraction of the way we do things at St Jude's is its immediacy. If someone wants to sponsor a child, there is no middle man, no central organisation. The money they send over goes directly to pay for that child's education, uniform, food and clothing. A big part of our work here is keeping sponsors informed about what their child is doing, with photographs, letters and reports. If they send their child a parcel, we send the sponsor a photograph of the child unwrapping the parcel. Many sponsors actually come over to St Jude's to stay and meet the child they are sponsoring – and a representative from the office will go with them to visit the child's family. It's a very direct, personal relationship in an age where large charities are sometimes viewed with suspicion by people who wonder whether their money is really going to the right place or paying some bureaucrat's salary back in Sydney. So all our public relations work is time-consuming but vital, both to spread the word to new people and to let those who are already involved with St Jude's know how they are making a difference.

Australian Story, with its tens of thousands of viewers, reached a whole new audience entirely. For my family, the repercussions from appearing on the program were more personal but no less important.

In a funny way, I think the program boosted my mother's confidence. When I married Richard and left Australia, part of Mum's concern was 'what people would say'. Rural communities can be very conservative and gossipy and I am sure there were a few of stories doing the rounds about Sue's daughter going off and marrying a black man and living in the wilderness. In their minds, I was sharing a mud hut with chickens and a primitive husband, most likely with a bone through his nose. If they thought about the school at all, it was probably to imagine a couple of thatched humpies with a few children learning their alphabets. When *Australian Story* came out, suddenly the people back home could see for themselves what all of my letters home or even photographs hadn't been able to convey.

St Jude's was not just scraping along the bottom. It was a fine school, with wonderful facilities – computers, playing fields and a library – and exceptionally bright, gorgeous children, a school that could stand with pride anywhere. The area where I lived was lush and beautiful, my husband was handsome and supportive. Mum's phone rang off the hook!

Our relationship too, which had improved markedly ever since Mum had first seen and fallen in love with the children, received another boost from the program. While we'd never completely fallen out – both of us had too much love and respect for each other for that – I had always felt hurt that she had never accepted Richard or our marriage. It was pointless to dwell unduly on the fact that this meant my father had never seen where I lived or what I'd achieved with the school but it was a lingering source of regret to me.

But as I saw my mother's pride in St Jude's grow, I saw that she also now understood that my marriage was an integral part of the school's success. Without Richard, there would be no St Jude's. From that moment on, Mum began to ask after Richard with real warmth and interest in her voice when she called, almost as if she were speaking about one of her own boys. She's now planning to visit us in Africa, which would mean so much to me.

It was a milestone too in my changing relationship with my brothers. Until they watched the program, they hadn't realised how tough it had been for me to leave and get married in the face of my family's disapproval. Nick, in particular, was reduced to tears by the program, saying to Paddy: 'We should have made a bit more of an effort and gone to the wedding.' To which Paddy – who'd been the one family representative at the wedding – replied unsympathetically: 'Yeah, you should have.'

But at the time, Nick had had young children and I'd completely understood his reasons for not making the long and expensive trip to Africa. It was more important for me that they were onside now. Benn too, who had been so set against my marrying Richard, now seemed to realise that he hadn't lost me to the wilds of Africa. I know he only took the stance he did because he loved me so much, but I am still the same Gemma he'd raced on bikes to catch the bus to school and gone with to B&Ss. I feel he is so relieved that I haven't changed and it's been so good to put it all behind us and get along as we always did when we were young. It's especially lovely to see our children together playing.

The response to *Australian Story* from people wanting to help, both as prospective sponsors and as volunteers, was extraordinary. There were 200 children we'd already selected for the school who immediately found sponsors. And for the first time ever, we had a list of 150 sponsors waiting to be assigned a child. In the short term, we could plan to start 150 new children at the beginning of 2006 – with all the associated building, staffing and transportation costs that would entail – but I also realised it was a priority to look at the long-term future of the school.

There were so many different directions we could go in and I wanted to take them all. For a long time, I'd recognised that we were going to have to open a secondary school in 2009, when our first set of children would reach that stage. In Tanzania, primary school goes up to Grade 7, when there's another set of state-wide external examinations. Most children at government schools will fail this exam but even the ones who pass aren't guaranteed a place at a government high school. There are just too few schools for the number of children.

My plan, then, was to continue on with our oldest class as they moved through the grades. When they were ready for high school, we had to be ready with a high school for them. Originally, I'd thought we could add the high school onto our existing campus. Remembering my father's dictum: 'Buy any piece of land you can afford – without it, you can't do anything,' over the years I've bought a patchwork of land around us, which has enabled us to build more classrooms, playing fields and accommodation for volunteers and visitors. There was a spare field behind our banana plantation that I'd thought would be just the spot for a secondary campus, but that was when I'd envisaged having only two streams at each level throughout the school. Well, in 2005 we had six streams in Standard 2 and counting, so it was obvious we were soon going to burst out of our Moshono land.

What we needed to do was duplicate the school and build another, on a different block of land somewhere else, still in the vicinity of Arusha and preferably at the base of Mount Meru, where the need was so great. Almost half our children came from that area and their lives would be a lot easier if they didn't have to travel the half hour or more out to Moshono each day. Eventually, we'd want to duplicate every class on each campus so that both went all the way through from kinder to Year 12, servicing their immediate area. This second campus has to be running by the start of 2008.

Another priority for us was to build a boarding school. I'd had parents asking me for a long time about providing boarding facilities but I'd always been hesitant. Running the school with normal hours was time-consuming enough – having children here for 24 hours a day, seven days a week could be the stuff of nightmares. But there certainly was a need. Some of the children had such a long way to travel each day. All of them were from poor backgrounds but some had to return home each day to conditions that would challenge even the most dedicated student. We had a lot of children who could benefit from a safe, stable environment where they could get on with their work and be supplied with good, nutritious food outside the school lunch we already provided.

To take one example – there was a little boy, Bart, who lived with his grandmother and younger sister because his mother, who looked like she was about 13, had been unable to care for them. Grandma's 'house' was a lean-to humpy measuring about two metres by one. There was certainly no money for a kerosene lamp by which to do homework or even enough to buy a regular supply of candles. We'd arranged for Bart to go to a nearby house each evening to complete his homework but really, expecting a kid from that sort of background to turn up clean and on time every day, in a complete uniform with his work done, was a big ask. And Bart's situation was by no means unique.

Another child, Mary Michael, was investigated by one of the Parents' Committee who suspected that her home life was less than supportive. Mary Michael is one of three children by three different fathers and when the parent representative went to her house to assess conditions, Mary's mother was – how should I put this? – *entertaining* a stranger in front of the children. How can a child under such conditions perform her best at school?

Yet another: Martha Afrael's father moved for work but wanted his daughter to stay in school. So he expected her to walk more than ten kilometres each morning to the bus stop. Having to start walking at 4.00 am was too much for the child, so another family offered to host her totally free of charge until the boarding school is completed in 2007.

Yes, we needed a boarding house.

So these were my next two goals: expanding into secondary schooling and boarding. I knew that neither was going to be cheap, so we needed some major infrastructure support for the school. New sponsors were coming in at the same rate as new children, which was fantastic. But these bigger projects demanded a whole new infrastructure. With the original School of St Jude we've just added bit by bit when we could afford to – and sometimes when we couldn't. But to build a new campus in its entirety, we'd have to have the money upfront to buy the land, pay the builders, staff the school from scratch, and buy a new fleet of buses. I had no idea how we were going to come up with it.

Then came the invitation I needed: to address a Rotary conference in the United States. I was invited by the Rushmore Rapid City Rotary Club, South Dakota, who very kindly sent me $2000 for the ticket. I managed to get one for $1600 and immediately emailed other friends in America and asked how far I could go with the remaining $400. How close is Texas to Rushmore? Answer: not very, but it's a lot closer than Africa. In the end, a woman called Cindy Skarbek, from a wonderful family, took over my itinerary and made me keep the $400 for expenses.

Cindy flew me to the Grapevine and Wichita Falls Rotary clubs in Texas, where there were already ten or so sponsors living. It was so good being able to meet these people in the flesh when I already knew their names by heart and was able to tell them all about their sponsored children. Then I went to Boston, where I had a few days with Tom and Judy Wagner, who had been a great help to the school's development ever since Tom had driven the little blue bus. We had a terrific slide show night with some of their friends and it was lovely to spend time with the two of them.

But my final and most significant stop was in Washington DC, where I was to meet Cindy's parents, Gordon and Helen Smith, who unbeknown to me would make a big financial commitment to the building program at St Jude's. The Smiths had been in Tanzania in 2004 with my friend Buck Tilley, the boss of Thompson's Safari Company. Buck is a tremendous supporter of the school and whenever he can he always recommends our school to interested clients and shows them what we're doing. I had met the Smiths' son Bruce in Tanzania but it was so nice to meet the rest of his family in person.

People like the Wagners, the Smiths and other lovely families such as the Weinlands from New Jersey, the Cubits from Melbourne and the Campbells from Sydney are so precious because they really want to help make a difference for the children here in Tanzania. They never ask for anything in return and are always willing to listen and advise, which is incredibly valuable, given their combined business acumen. Having them around means that good advice is just on the other end of an email, especially at a time when I really miss my Dad. Their support means a tremendous amount to me and to everyone who is passionate about this school project – we all know that for the school to continue to help more and more children, the capital needs are huge and always growing.

The trip to the States and the Smiths' commitment of support set the tone for the rest of 2005. When I returned from America, it occurred to me that so much had happened to me and the school that I attributed to the watchful care of St Jude, but I hadn't done much to repay him, other than cuff him around the head when times were tough. We'd never even celebrated the poor man's feast day – 28 October – and I'd named the school after him.

Also, we'd spent so much time 'firefighting', bogged down in minor crises of one sort or another, that we'd never had an opportunity to stand back, look at the school and give thanks for what we'd all achieved. It was time to do just that, with a celebratory Feast of St Jude. I had an extra reason to be thankful – I'd managed to persuade poor Kim to return to us, disrupting her life terribly but making mine a thousand times easier.

Since I've lived here, I've had a few people question my faith in St Jude and religion in general, asking me whether it's been tested by the suffering I see in Africa on a daily basis. I drive past tiny villages of mud huts barely tall enough to accommodate a standing adult, and each village will have a tiny wooden church out of which comes the most glorious singing. People in Africa might suffer materially but they don't suffer spiritually, unlike us in the West. I actually think that heaven is going to be full of people from third-world countries because they never had the material temptations of people in the first world.

When I look back at when Richard and I were first married, before we had electricity or running water, things were so much simpler. I'd be cooking for Richard, waiting for him to come home. When he did, we'd share our meat and rice by the light of a candle. It was really lovely. How important are the things that we in the West think are necessary for our happiness? Nike shoes or $300 jeans? They're certainly not going to get you to heaven before an African woman who's lived a good life and has struggled but given thanks for what she's got.

Before I came out here, I believed in God implicitly but in an automatic sort of way, and also out of a quite childish fear of hell and purgatory. But since I've been in Africa, I've felt the presence of God as a reality and my religion is much more real to me, even though I don't make it to mass quite so often. I know I'm a bit excessive about St Jude, but I really feel he listens to me and that the school wouldn't have developed as it had if he hadn't thought it was the right thing for me to do. If I look at all the coincidences that have shaped the path I've trodden, I'm convinced that St Jude was guiding me along the way. Why did I not get into medicine, going instead into teaching? Why didn't I die on the ferry? There are millions of great men in this country – why did I meet the one who had a father who not only believed in education but had a spare piece of land to give me? Why did my husband happen to be fantastic with vehicles and cars and able to maintain a fleet of nineteen buses? Why is he one of the rare African men who doesn't try to force his wife into a mould but lets me go my own way?

For me, there are too many coincidences. I'm almost looking forward to the day I die so that I can finally meet St Jude and run through my notes with him and ask: 'Was this because of you? Did you make this happen or was that just my imagination?'

In the meantime, we owed him a celebration and that's what we gave him. It was the most beautiful day. In the morning, we had a thanksgiving service, thanking everyone whose contributions enabled our school to function: the sponsors, the donors, the teachers, the cooks, the cleaners, the drivers, the parents. Even though all our children are very poor, everyone had to bring something to the service, so they brought eggs and sugar, rice and fruit, chickens and even pairs of shoes. Then we sorted all the goods and gathered them up in buckets to distribute to the children at an orphanage outside town, the poor old people in the slums and the people who stay for long periods in the hospitals. The children were so proud to be helping others, they were just beaming with happiness.

Then in the afternoon we had a concert, with every class putting on a performance, on the stage we'd made in the hall we'd built ourselves. The girls from one class did an African dance and the boys – because their teacher was a New Zealander – did a Maori haka. The little kindergarteners did a gorgeous song about animals on a mountain. And 3B – who won the prize for the best performance of the day – put on the play *Danny in the Toy Box*, by Richard Tulloch, an Australian playwright who'd been out earlier in the year and worked with the children on storytelling.

I couldn't possibly have been more proud – nor could the children or their teachers.

The Feast Day of St Jude was such a success that it made me think about our Standard 4s, who were approaching their end-of-year external examinations. Reaching the end of Standard 4 was a big milestone, not only for the 27 children who'd worked so hard, but for us, because it was the first year that we were able to put children up for the exam. The results were going to be very important for us. In our own minds, we were achieving great things with the children, but only the results would tell us whether that was borne out in practice.

In preparation, the children had had a series of trial exams. Our school is part of Ward 27, which comprises seven schools, or about 560 Standard 4 children. We had to send a teacher along to another school to mark their papers and, in return, a teacher from a third school came here to mark our papers. It was all a little chaotic and we had to collate all the results from the ward because we were the only ones who could put them on a spreadsheet, but the results were unequivocal. In the mock exams, every child from St Jude's passed. Not only that, but the top 22 places in the ward were taken by St Jude's children. It wasn't the real thing, but it was certainly cause for optimism.

So when the Standard 4s completed their real exams – all of them completely confident of their brilliance, of course – we decided to celebrate their 'graduation' with a day out at a national park and then a formal graduation ceremony.

I took the kids with their teachers to Lake Manyara – a beautiful national park particularly well known for its hippos, flamingos, elephants and tree-climbing lions – and we had a great day out. The children, released from their weeks of studying, were in top form; even the normally quiet and studious ones, like Athumani and Esuvat or my lovely head girl, Anna, were shrieking and singing and jumping up and down in their seats. I knew there was no way I was going to keep this energetic mob cooped up for four hours in the bus, so at the gate I asked whether there was a picnic site in the park, somewhere the children could get out and run around. Sure thing, the men at the gate answered, just let them out at the hippo pool.

So after a wonderful hour spotting elephants and giraffes, when the children were getting a bit restless, I asked them: 'Who wants to see a hippo?'

'Me!' 'Me!' 'I do!' came the chorus. We took them to the hippo pool and, sure enough, it was full of the seemingly placid but actually very dangerous creatures. We kept our distance but the children were able to stretch their legs and get their wriggles out.

Suddenly, a thunderous-looking National Parks official appeared out of nowhere. 'What are you doing? There are lions just behind here. The children could be killed – and so could you.'

'But the man at the gate said we could get out at the hippo pool,' I said.

'Not here – over there,' he said, pointing to another clearing about 400 metres away.

'Sorry,' I said. 'Come on, kids.' And we packed up and moved our things around to the picnic site. Later on in the afternoon, when we'd stopped for afternoon tea at another picnic site, a couple of young National Parks guards approached some of the children and teachers. I could see our social studies teacher deep in conversation and assumed the guard must have been a friend of hers.

When we got on the bus, the guards did too. I could hear them talking in rapid-fire Swahili to the teachers but couldn't quite follow what they were saying. One of the teachers translated: 'He says that he has a report that our bus was seen with the children illegally getting out of the vehicle and that there was a $500 fine. But don't worry,' she added. 'We've all told him that the report is wrong and we certainly didn't do that. We were in the bus the whole time except when they saw us at the picnic site.'

I took over and explained that, yes, we had got out at the wrong place but it had been a simple misunderstanding and we corrected it as soon as we'd discovered our error.

'A mistake?' the guard asked.

'Yes, a mistake,' I said. 'Sorry.'

'Oh, well, that's all right, then.' And off they went.

When they'd gone I tried to talk to the teachers, to make them see how wrong and unnecessary it was to lie, especially in front of the children. I could see I was making no headway until I mentioned: 'And we were in the school bus too.'

Ah yes, they cried. How could we be so silly? Of course they'd catch us out in a bus with 'School of St Jude' written on all sides in primary colours.

They'd missed the main point about honesty and setting ethical standards but at that point I gave up. As I had realised by this time, Africa would not change overnight.

The graduation ceremony was the culmination of years of hard work for my dear Standard 4s. In ten years we probably won't be making such a fuss about completing a set of primary school exams, but that first class was very special. I really wanted the children and their parents to know how wonderful we thought they were and to have a real bigwig as a special guest at their graduation to confirm their importance. I'd heard that the local District Commissioner, a Mr Elias Lali, was a man of about 55. Perfect for Kim to go and work her special magic on. He's a big man around here – sort of like a state premier – and he's driven around in a brand-new Land Cruiser with tinted windows and a flag. He's so important that you rarely see him.

'Kim,' I said, thrusting a tube of lipstick at her. 'Don't come back to this school till you've pinned him down. We've got ten days between the children finishing their exams and the end of the school year. Instead of asking if he can come on a particular day, which he can easily refuse, ask him to give us two hours any time he chooses and we'll fit in around him. Then he can't say he's fully booked.'

Kim went off to do battle and texted me later that afternoon with a message that read: 'Friday 25th, between 10 and 1.'

It was a great achievement to have him there and it made the parents, teachers and children so much more proud than if we'd just had the local mayor in attendance. All the younger children in the school came to the ceremony, giving them a glimpse of what their future held, inspiring them to strive even harder. Of course, there were a few mishaps. We'd planned the ceremony beautifully but then had one of our inexplicable power cuts. No electricity, so no mikes for our dignitaries or the children.

But the children didn't need any artificial amplification. Anna and Athumani, our head girl and boy, presented a speech that they'd written with their classmates' help. Their clear young voices carried confidently on the air through the hall. Just under four years ago, they'd started at the school with little English and even less hope. Now they were addressing an assembly of hundreds of parents and friends, fluently and proudly, with their heads high and their eyes on the future.

I know how I felt hearing them. I can only imagine how proud their parents must have been.

'First of all,' Athumani said. 'We would like to thank you all for joining us in this very special day in our lives, on a special way to you, Mr Elias, our District Commissioner. We know that as Government Leader you have a lot to do, but you have set aside these three hours to come and be with us. We are really grateful. We would also like to thank the District Education Officer

Mr Lema for being with us today. To all our guests, we say, welcome to St Jude's School and feel at home.'

Anna took over and they alternated in this way for the rest of the speech. 'Our school is growing very fast and we are sure it is going to become one of the greatest schools of its kind in this continent and when God wishes we would also be among the greatest people of this continent.

'Welcome, our parents, and feel that you are at home. We would like to thank the school board and the school Parents' Committee for leading our school to this great success.

'Thank you, our teachers, for your great effort in educating us in a very special and good way, we cannot pay you for what you have done to us. We only ask God to bless you. We also say thanks to all school workers for helping us to reach this stage.

'To you, Mrs Richard, we cannot find enough words to thank you. You left home and came to help us. We are now able to stand here and talk with confidence, we are sure of our future and this is because of you, Mrs Richard. We promise that we won't let you down. We are sure of getting good grades in the national examination we have done just a few days ago. Thank you very much. May God bless you.

'We thank the donors and our sponsors for paying for all our education requirements, for us to learn and have a chance in our lives. Thank you very much and may God bless you all.

'As the highest class in this school, we advise all St Jude's pupils to work very hard in their lessons as the only way of paying back this great help we are getting.

'Once again, we thank you very much for coming and please feel at home.

'May God bless you all.'

The applause was a solid wall in the open hall, and the children's cheers rang out to Mount Meru.

EPILOGUE

January 2006

The new year has started and the madness has begun again. Only a couple of years ago when we began the school year with around 100 students and five staff, it was chaos. Children were milling everywhere and some had to be plucked out of the wrong class-rooms mid-lesson. Now, although we have nearly 700 students and about 150 staff, both academic and support, the first day of school went off beautifully. The only thing that was lost was my voice from directing the troops.

The builders and carpenters have done an amazing job through the holidays, sleeping at the school and working in shifts, and, miraculously, our new block of eight classrooms was finished ahead of schedule. Teams of volunteers visited over the break, assembling and painting playground equipment. Our wonderful academic master, Nestory Msoffe, and the school's deputy, Ben Mainga, devoted their own time to working out programs for the new members of staff and I'm so hoping that the new staff will slot in more easily than some have in previous years.

We've always had a few teething problems when new staff come in from other African schools. They bring their own school culture with them and have to learn new ways – especially how to discipline children without resorting to the stick or the sly pinch under the desk. Our level of computerisation is also difficult for a lot of them, but we've got ongoing training and mentorship programs and, for me, educating the educators is just as important as teaching the children.

There are nearly 200 new children in Standard 1 and 2. The ones who had completed their probationary period at the end of last year came last week to be fitted for their new uniforms. It was complete mayhem but, at the same time, it's always beautiful, almost ceremonial, seeing the children shedding their old selves and trying on their new identity. They arrived in the usual eclectic assortment of second-hand clothes from the market and locally made outfits. Little girls were dressed in what looked like taffeta party-dresses, complete with puff-sleeved bolero jackets. The boys wore thick woollen jumpers, batik shirts and shorts. One was sporting a T-shirt emblazoned with a shamrock and the words 'Proud to be Irish'. All were completely gorgeous, from their close-cropped or braided heads to their toes. Whoever said 'There's no such thing as an ugly child' must have been thinking of African children.

Within a couple of hours, this motley assortment was transformed into a cohesive group of beautifully neat St Jude's students, beside themselves with pride in their navy uniforms, their hats at the correct angle, their black school shoes shiny. By simply donning a uniform a child's whole persona changes from quiet and shy to proud and confident, with head held high. It's not like the selection process, where you have to choose which students to keep and which to send away. This is one of the most rewarding parts of admitting new students. It's wonderful to see the joy on their faces and their parents', and know that we're in this community together for the long haul, all the way through to the end of secondary school.

Getting started on the construction of the secondary school will be the big priority this year. It will need to be ready for our first class of children in 2009. And we've now bought the right block of land for a boarding house, just a ten-minute walk from the school, so we need to get straight onto plans for a building with dormitories, kitchens, bathrooms, study rooms, and rooms for play to open in 2007. So it's going to be a busy year. At the same time, the existing school continues to grow. We used to be contacted by a new sponsor maybe every two weeks or so. Now, we'd be getting a new sponsor every day. That means that every 25 days, on average, we need a new classroom, a new teacher, half a new bus.

We also have to start building a second primary school and secondary school, which will be on our second campus about 20 minutes away, as we are bursting at the seams at our current campus and will have troubles taking in next year's 200 new children, let alone all those in the years to come. The new campus at Usa River village will comprise primary, secondary and boarding, with the primary school and boarding house due to open in 2008, followed by the secondary school, which needs to open in 2009, at the same time as the secondary school at the current Moshono campus. Such big capital development but, with the help of people from all over the world, we are determined to succeed. At our Friday testings we are now getting more than 2000 children coming to the interviews with usually fewer than 20 gaining a place. Competition is fierce and the need is massive. I am sure we could have ten schools around the Arusha city area and still be a long way from filling the demand. We still have to have a one-child-per-family policy, but imagine if one day we could have a two-children-per-family policy. Better still, no limits at all. We have a LOT to do to give the children here in Tanzania just a fraction of the opportunities taken for granted by a Western child.

When I think of all that's facing me, I do worry that I've bitten off more than I can chew. I often have people saying to me, and I'm sure they mean it kindly: 'Gemma, I think you're going too fast. Just slow down. Maybe you should stop taking new children and just concentrate on the ones you've got now.'

I can see why they are saying it but I don't think I could face God if I did that. If we said we weren't going to take any new children for the next six months, what if a girl like Jesca was the one who missed out on a place? Imagine if it was Erick who takes the chalk around, Athumani who *will* be a pilot someday or Alex Elifas, who's jumped two classes since he came here.

People in this country spend their lives hoping to find someone who'll help to pay for their school fees so they have a chance of a better life. If I have sponsors lined up, waiting in the wings, and a bright, needy child waiting to be educated, how wrong would it be of me to say that I couldn't bring them together just because I didn't yet have the infrastructure in place? It's my duty to get my butt into gear, get that infrastructure up and make sure that the management side is working, so that we *can* take those children and match them with a willing sponsor so as not to turn away anyone who deserves a place.

I have other people saying to me: 'What is it that drives you? What keeps you going?' as if there's some magic formula that makes us able to achieve what we have here. I wish there was but the dull truth is, it's just hard work: getting up in the morning, seeing what needs to be done, putting one foot in front of the other and completing that task, then beginning the next one. It *is* difficult living here and doing what I do. It's a million times tougher than I could have imagined. But that's what makes anything we achieve so much more gratifying.

For me, the challenge brings out the full force of my competitive nature. Last year we had one Standard 4 class. This year we'll have five. When we have two campuses, we'll be churning out many more classes of Standard 4 every year. I don't think I'll ever rest until we have campuses across at least East Africa and I honestly don't see why that couldn't work. I truly believe that education is the only reliable way out of poverty and you can't wait for things to happen at a government level. Sometimes you just have to do them yourself.

Because we live here and we are on the ground, I am confident that we can keep our organisation direct and accountable no matter how big it grows. Even now, our sponsors receive as detailed information about their child as they did when there were only three students at the school. We know every child here intimately and I can't see that changing.

St Jude's is an obsession for me, which is a bit of a problem, but it's what drives me. Other people seem able to switch on and off and manage to have a life outside, but at some level I'm thinking about the school 24 hours a day. Thank God for my family because I don't have a social life. But underneath it all, I really do love it. I love getting into my office every morning and reading my emails. I love forward-planning. I love fundraising. The training I'm receiving here, that everyone involved with the school is receiving, is just the extreme sport to end all extreme sports. Every bit of me feels that it's utilised and stretched and challenged. I couldn't have imagined this future for myself when I was growing up, but with hindsight I realise I've chosen the perfect vocation that I'd unwittingly been training for all my life.

I compare that to how it feels when I go back to Australia and, while there's a whole level of comfort there that I'm missing out on, it all feels so safe and controlled that I don't know if I could live like that anymore. I really notice the preoccupation with safety when I'm in Australia. There are whole shops devoted to, for example, protective clothing. The people are so cautious and law-abiding. It makes it harder to have the grand vision, to go for broke and take a chance.

One of the great things about living in Africa is you can say, 'To hell with the rules!' If I want to put up a building, I pace out the dimensions myself. To decide where the windows should go, I wander around with a piece of chalk and mark them out. I'm completely free, not bound by someone else's idea of what you can or can't do. When you're not worried about what other people are saying, you begin to think only in terms of *how* you can make your dreams reality, not whether or not those dreams are realistic.

It's hard to step back and look at the big picture sometimes. I'm able to on occasions like the St Jude's thanksgiving day or the Standard 4 graduation, but mostly the joys I get are small everyday joys. This morning Athumani came in to see me and said: 'I hear that you called me.' He was so serious and such a little old man. I just thought, *Oh, you are so very cute.* And I get countless lovely cards from the children, saying, 'Thank you, Mrs Richard, for our new bus,' or 'Thank you for fixing our swings.' I'll see the pride and amazement on a parent's face as they hear for the first time their child communicating in a different language. When you're up to your neck in paperwork, these are little reminders of why exactly you're doing what you're doing.

I get such a thrill from a great many things. One of the biggest buzzes is when sponsors come over to visit and meet the child they've been sponsoring. I remember when Athumani's sponsors, Mr and Mrs Conroy, came out on the first tour group we organised as a fundraiser for the school. The morning after they arrived, they were watching the children stepping off the buses. I pointed Athumani out to them and they raced up and gave him the biggest hug. There were tears all round and it was just beautiful. It seems to me to be a miraculous thing, bringing together a couple from Brisbane and a boy from Moshono village with a common purpose.

I don't have any illusions that I'm going to change the world. I'm not even going to change Tanzania. I think my outlook is quite realistic by now. I just focus on the few children whose lives I can change. If I can help our head girl, Anna, who started out as a frightened, abused young girl from the Kenyan border, achieve her dream of becoming a teacher, then that will make my day. If she happens to become headmistress of a school, that would be even better, but I'm not expecting her to become Minister for Education and change the system. If one day I hop on a plane and the captain's voice is Athumani's, I'll be ecstatic. Even if I go into the hardware shop and some of the boys working there are old St Jude's kids, I'd be thrilled.

Basically, if these St Jude's kids have a better future than they would have had, whatever direction that takes them, then we've succeeded. If they can find good employment, save a little, buy a little bit of land, keep themselves in better health, help their guardians, parents or grandparents, that's a great outcome and all we can hope for.

But for the moment, my future hopes are more specific: I'm just waiting for the mail to bring the results of the Standard 4 exams. Every time the post comes, I have butterflies. I was so confident but now I'm nervous that they won't do as well as they'd expected after the mock exams. They'll be so disappointed, not only the children but all the people who put such a lot of effort into helping them. The teachers who stayed late to provide extra tutoring, the bus drivers who had to provide extra runs in the evening, even the cooks and the cleaners who cheerfully put in extra hours to help the children achieve their best results.

I have to repeat to myself: 'Results aren't everything, results aren't everything.' But really, I know that at this stage that they are, if not everything, then something pretty important. The children's sense of pride and achievement is riding on them. The parents are watching, the sponsors are watching, other schools in the district are watching. Knowing within ourselves that we're on the right track is one thing, but how will we measure up in the eyes of the outside world?

And they're here! This morning the envelope arrived from the Ministry of Education. I ripped it open and gulped the news down greedily, then went back to the beginning and tried to read slowly, to make sense of it all, with my heart racing. When I was sure I had everything straight in my mind, I yelled to whoever was in a one-kilometre radius:

'Come and hear this!!! We've got the results!!! They're unbelievable!!!'

Out of 204 schools in our district, both private and state, St Jude's came *third*! It's better than my wildest imaginings.

Not only has every child passed, but even the one who gained the lowest mark of the class still was placed in the top 20 percent of the district. Out of our 27 beautiful Standard 4 children, 19 scored 100 percent in at least one subject.

I could not be prouder of them all. Given that it's the first year St Jude's has ever attempted the Tanzanian national exams, given that half the time we were all operating by guesswork, in the dark, the whole class's results are beyond anything I'd dreamed of.

And then, to top it off, there are the individual achievements. Out of more than 17,000 children in the area, we had the student who beat them all: sweet, studious Esuvat Ojungo. Another four were in the top 10 for their sex. Dear Alex Elifas, who always brings a smile to my face, came fifth. Cecilia Benedict, so confident and grown-up, was eighth. Eliudi William has surprised himself – as usual – by coming ninth. And this is an honour he shares with my lovely, serious head boy, soon to be pilot, Athumani Hamedi.

Those gorgeous children, whom I last saw kicking a ball around in the playground, are well on their way to a bright, open future.

When these children started at the school, we had only a few staff and no experience with the Tanzanian educational system. Our entire school measured half an acre. The system for selecting children was still in its infancy, the sponsorship scheme just beginning.

At every step of the way, these children have been the guinea pigs as we experimented and expanded and made countless mistakes. And still they've thrived, due to their innate intelligence and industry and the very special magic of St Jude's.

I can't help but think that if this is what we can achieve, at this early stage in what I pray will be a long existence for the school, just imagine what the future will hold! If we continue receiving the incredible support we get from people from all around the world, I think we can achieve anything.

Forget what I said before – maybe we *can* change the world.

To find out more about The School of St Jude, please go to our website <www.schoolofstjude.co.tz> or email us at <school ofstjude@habari.co.tz>.

Our website contains lots of information about visiting us, volunteering, donating to the school and contributing to sponsorship programs. Plus we have lots of regularly updated photographs. Every month we send out an online newsletter; if you would like to receive it, please send us an email with 'Subscribe to Newsletter' in the title.

We have also recently established an association called 'Friends of St Jude's'. The members organise events and invite their friends – the aim is not to fundraise but to spread the word about the school. Anyone can belong, so if you are interested please send us an email with 'Friends of St Jude's' in the title and include your postal address, and we'll send you out a 'Friend's Pack'.

For any enquiries in regards to:

- Events and brochure/book/DVD requests,
  Contact: Dale Dawes
  Email: schoolofstjude@bigpond.com
  Phone: (+61) 4 1452 1802 [between the hours of 8am and 8pm only]
- Sponsorships, general donations, becoming a Friend of St Jude's or visiting the school, please contact Gemma directly:
  Email: schoolofstjude@habari.co.tz
  Phone: Int'l – (+255) 756 236 330 or 754 566 136
          Local – 0756 236 330 or 0754 566 136
  Address: The School of St Jude, PO Box 11875, Arusha, Tanzania, East Africa